LISTEN UP!

THE VETERANS' WRITING GROUP
GROUP
SAN DIEGO COUNTY

Listen Up! This book has been given to you because of generous donations to the Veterans' Writing Group of San Diego. Enjoy it and pass it along to other veterans.

Book design by Ron Pickett

ISBN-13: 978-1984062789
ISBN-10: 1984062786
BISAC: History / Essays

Veterans' Writing Group San Diego County offers mentorship, support and publishing opportunities for veteran writers of all skill levels.

www.veteranswritinggroup.org

DEDICATION

LISTEN UP!, the second book published by the Veterans' Writing Group, is humbly dedicated to three of our writers whom we have lost since the publication of *Away For The Holidays*: Dolph Brostrom, Bud Parson, and Terry Severhill.

- Dolph inspired us because of his energy, enthusiasm, and dedication to his writing.
- Bud amazed us with the emotion of his poetry and ability to recall past events.
- Terry motivated us, thanks to his vibrant personality, his focus on writing, his poetry performance skills, and his support for emerging writers.

All three of these great men made significant contributions to our group and our members.

Fair winds and following seas.

TABLE OF CONTENTS

INTRODUCTION

Listen Up! is the second book published by the Veterans' Writing Group (VWG). The success of our first book, *Away for the Holidays*, encouraged these prolific, talented authors to share their insights, experiences, and creativity again.

Whether it's a four-year hitch or a 26-year career, military life can be a writer's haven, supplying as it does boundless material for compelling, thought-provoking, and often humorous tales. For *Listen Up!,* the authors were tasked to write stories about what they took away from their time as service members. It's a broad topic, and the authors interpreted it through both prose and poetry. Common themes that emerged are lessons learned, human nature better understood, and extraordinary circumstances resulting in maturity quickly supplanting naïveté.

We hope you enjoy these stories, and encourage veterans interested in writing to join us. We meet the first Saturday of every month at Veterans Association of North County in Oceanside, California. Our mission is to provide a safe and supportive environment for our writers, some of whom are beginners and some of whom are published authors.

Thanks to generous donations from the San Diego Board of Supervisors, the Issa Foundation, and individuals, as well as revenue from book sales, we donated over 1,600 copies of *Away for the Holidays* to a variety of local veterans' and active duty military organizations, including the U.S. Naval Hospitals at Balboa and Camp Pendleton, USO San Diego, and VA hospitals throughout the county. We hope to do the same with *Listen Up!* Copies of both books are available for purchase on Createspace and Amazon.com. This book owes its existence in no small part to the time and talent selflessly devoted to its production by VWG's resident expert on publication, Ron Pickett. His enthusiasm and attention to detail made this all possible.

Gail Chatfield
Co-Founder, Veterans Writing Group

PROLOGUE

Listen Up!
Tom Calabrese

You may discover value in this book,
You may, too, find the pictures worth a look;
Whether we be Red, White, Blue, or Green,
Army, Navy, Air Force, or Marine,
All agree no matter how you spin it,
Life can change in less than a minute.

As long as the flag waves and eagles fly,
Americans will turn our eyes to the sky;
Duty calls and we leave for hostile land
To confront evil and make our stand.

Some take the same path yet end with different views,
Others take different paths yet find the same clues;
Just as we heeded those who preceded us,
We hope those who follow us listen up!

These tales aren't about heroes and glory,
Just men and women sharing their stories;
So too we, VWG, of North County,
Wish you all the best with your own story.

The Learning Curve Sometimes Looks Like a Cliff
By Terry Severhill

Time: midmorning, midweek, spring, 1970
Place: Boonies, Quang Tri Province, RVN

I learned that grown men need to cry but don't.
I learned that boys who are grown men, who are more
experienced, still do stupid things.
I learned that being in charge isn't all that it's cracked up to be.
That being in charge is not a guarantee that everything will turn
out okay.
That death doesn't choose, doesn't care.
I learned that death comes to us all.
That being in charge is to be responsible,
And that can really suck.

The following poem among the first, probably the third, written
after returning to the world, about January or February 1971.

PATROL LEADER

Dignitaries come.
Fame?
Not even fifteen minutes.
Hero! They cry.
Speech, speech shouts the crowd.
I smile, a little nervous.
Speech! The clamor grows.
I feel a chill in the wind, pause...head bowed in thought.
It is an ungodly heat; searing, scorching our bare backs.
Drenched in sweat our fouled clothes cling to our limbs, fatigued,
weary.
The air suffocating.
The putrid stench of decaying, fermented foliage violates our
nostrils.

Our eyes, blue or brown patches in rings of fire.
The mud is wed to our boots, there is a sluching sound as we pry our feet
From the titan grip of slime.
Tentacles from our bodies sway.
Thick black leeches devouring thin blood.
Vampires, wingless bats from a wet hell.
Straps cut deep into lean, chaffed shoulders threatening to sever arms from tired bodies.
Skin worn raw smarts from running sweat.
Bites from a thousand flying teeth tattoo our faces.
A thin sound.
A silent sound.
A dreaded sound.
An angel in agony cries,
Banshees shriek, a thousand damned souls scream and descend upon us.

INCOMING! I shout, but there is no need. They, like me, have already
Sought the meager shelter of wet muck and newly-planted rice.
CRUMP!
The first shell shatters, exploding, leaving its load of near death and pain.
Like some biblical flood,
A rain seeks to drown us with drops made of steel.
The ground heaves, bucks, an earthen sea, a rice paddy quake.

Giant fists slamming into yielding dirt.
Crump! Crump! Faster, nearer, farther.
The earth is shoveled up in great heaps of smoldering crud.
Shallow pits, self-emptied graves.
I seek to push, dig, wedge myself deeper into the vile scum.
Seconds like hours drag by reluctantly, slowly as if to add to our punishment
In this, our very own Grand Inquisition.
Panic lurks close at hand.
Despair seeps into my mind.

Terror clutches at my heart, threatening to stop it.
The shelling continues, the Devil's concerto,
Satan's symphony.
Forcing me to seek refuge in the odious ooze,
Sweeping all reluctance from my mind.
Cool,
Wet.
Dark,
A new womb.
Protection.
Time passes.
An eerie quite settles upon us.
Our ears deafened to the pain filled sobs escaping trembling lips of
conquered bodies.
I survey the arena with mud-encrusted face.
I see sights which sicken my calloused conscience.
Unimagined horrors await my eyes as the last shadows of death
are
Swept away in a half-hearted breeze.

Broken, twisted bodies, split upon the now unquivering ground,
Tossed about as though they were some giant child's ragdolls,
Entrails like sawdust strewn upon the ground.
Careful I walk, so as not to step unwittingly
On some severed hand or slice of butchered flesh.
I walk to a reluctant corpse, eyes glazed, pleading to live, to linger
yet a while longer,
If only in agony, in this god forsaken hellhole rather than go into
the darkness.
I whisper Amen, but mean good-bye.
Another body not moving, eyes open, staring accusingly at me the
undead.
His mouth slightly open, a fly seeks passage.
More bodies, three together. I silently scream, (DON'T BUNCH UP!)
My hands are clenched tight.
My eyes seek some small hint of life, but as magnets to metal they
are drawn,
Drawn to spattered brains dripping from a crushed skull.

Blood seeps from an open chest and forms lakes of red-brown goo.
The third has no legs.
I have no tears to wash away the mud.
I glance at my watch, just moments, end to beginning to end.
I look at the sun, face twisted from its unyielding glare.
A small thought, unbidden, escapes my mind.
"Thank god it wasn't me."

Applause breaks into my secret hidden purgatory, and I look up.
"Say something!" the retired, silvered haired general growls.

I slowly walk to the microphone and say. . . . .
". . . . . Why is it Old Soldiers never die but the young go,
asking Why?"

* Not all the events described in this poem happened at the same
ambush. But over time the events, just as the lessons, have
merged, melded into one event.

Later:
I took what I had learned and strived to always be in charge. I
worked for over 30 years in the construction industry. I learned
every job from laborer to carpenter, to foreman, then job
superintendent, union electrician, safety coordinator and general
contractor. I always looked for any way to control the situation.
That by being in charge maybe I could prevent the past from
happening again. I also learned that if I am in charge of only me
then it doesn't matter if that guy messes up. No one else pays my
debt. Eventually, I learned to let others come up for air. It took me
years to come to the conclusion that I needn't control everyone all
the time. That just being in control of me, I was better off. Looking
back, I see this lesson over and over. Sometimes we aren't ready,
or we are unwilling to let go of the past.

Conclusion:

Not all lessons are correctly interpreted. Often, we over-compensate, trying to balance the books. Sometimes we learn the lesson more than once with different results.

The Three-Year-Old Farm Boy's Obsession
And the Captain's Voice!
By Joe Snyder

Have you ever seen an image of a three-year-old farm boy who keeps running toward airplane fly-overs just to watch them fly away and marvel? That's me of only 70 years ago! That three-year-old talked to himself, "When I grow up, I wanna be a pilot!" A pilot, really? How is there any correlation between the little farm boy and a pilot? "Impossible" – that will be the first thought that runs through most of our minds.

The answer is "YES." The connection is the United States Marine Corps! Oorahh!

It is the end of December 1965 and I have just graduated from college, i.e., The University of North Carolina at Chapel Hill. The war in Vietnam is heating up and the Army draft board is after my "you know what." The Marine Corps recruiter on Chapel Hill campus has already laid out the aviation program for me as a jarhead! I'm thrilled with the possibility to go to Navy flight school. I've decided to move forward with them before the Army approaches me.

The catch-22, however, was that I must go to Officer Candidate School first, get commissioned as a second lieutenant, and then go to Pensacola, Florida for Navy Flight training. I thought to myself, "Oh well, I can get through ten weeks of nonsense and then make my goal of learning to fly and get paid doing it...not a bad deal!" Besides, the dream of becoming a pilot is much bigger than catch-22. I picked up the phone and made an appointment for the initial interview.

The Recruiter who worked with my application was Captain Carl Mundy. He was my "Officer Selection Officer" and mentor before I left Chapel Hill for OCS. He told me how to prepare for the ten weeks ahead and to remember that "**I am the responsible person in charge of my own success.**"

So, I left Chapel Hill in early March 1966 on a flight to Washington, DC and a bus trip south to Quantico, Virginia, and Officer Candidate School. We were greeted by those "friendly" Drill Instructors (DIs) as they quickly organized us in marching groups and off we went.

During ten weeks of boot camp, we had to conquer 50 obstacles throughout the course, including hay bale jumps, tunnel crawls, hurdles, 6-foot vertical climbing walls, trenches, cargo net crawls, bridges, and push-up. DIs are at each station to make sure you've completed your obstacles.

The first two weeks, sometimes I hardly caught my breath. I commented to my partner comrade "what in the world have I got myself into?" Then the captain's voice came to me… "**I am the responsible person in charge of my own success**…moving on, Mr. Snyder."

The second half of boot camp, my physical strength improved dramatically. After familiarizing myself with the surroundings, I applied the captain's advice of running three miles every day. Every time I looked at my boots, I'm touched with how well he prepared his candidates. The captain saved my rear-end because, besides the above heavy exercises, all we did at OCS was run, run, and run some more every day.

No more exhaustion, no more being the last person crossing the finish line. At graduation, I'm a platoon honor candidate. During the graduation ceremony, I understood my success as one of the top officer candidates that mainly was supported by the captain's mantra. I figured it would be A MUST HAVE QUOTE that I will always carry with me, day and night.

I was commissioned as an Officer Second Lieutenant and given orders to report to NAS Pensacola for flight training. That was a big day in my life! The dream of a three-year-old farm boy came true. I'm now officially accepted to Naval Flight School. The bond is here – United States Marine Corps! Oorahh!

One beautiful afternoon in July 1967, the pinning-on of my gold wings as a naval aviator resulted in my promotion to first lieutenant. I'm blown away when the Naval Air Training Command admiral shook my hand and patted my shoulder, saying, "I'm so impressed with your aviation talents, you'll be a great pilot!" Again, the captain's voice "**I am the responsible person in charge of my own success**" is another confirmation of jar-head Joe Snyder's progressing military career.

I had orders to report to the commanding officer, Marine Helicopter Squadron HMM-161 at New River Marine Corps Air Station, North Carolina. This squadron was in "work up" to depart for operations in Southeast Asia in early 1968. That means "Go to War."

Upon arriving at my first official command squadron HMM-161, I was very fervent about the future of my service. I was also assigned to work with the new CH-46 twin turbine helo. This new aircraft was to replace the older H-34 that had been flying in Vietnam since 1965.

I started out as a co-pilot while learning the insides and outs of this bird, including its high-powered engines, rotors, hydraulics, speed, ability to land, taxi in the water, hovering capacity, combat support, search and rescue, rearming points, aero-medical evacuation of casualties from the field, and recovery of aircraft and personnel. My goal was to become an aircraft Commander before we left for NAM.

I worked very hard; grabbing every flight I could to master this bird. The aircraft (A/C) crew performance and survival really depended on my expertise. I was the first person present and the last person to leave at our training facility every day. Anytime I faced a setback, the captain's mantra came up immediately... "**I am the responsible person in charge of my own success.**"

My goal was met! I was designated as the HAC – Helicopter Aircraft Commander after completing six months training. On 20 April 1968, we departed MCAF New River with 24 aircraft heading for the West Coast where we would board the USS Princeton Aircraft carrier for the 17 days voyage to Southeast Asia and Vietnam. As novices and relentless young men, none of us realized what danger is waiting ahead for us; instead, we all felt very excited...about this "war" thing.

We landed off the shores of northern South Vietnam and offloaded to our new home at the Quang Tri Air Base about 12 miles south of the DMZ. We began to fly combat missions just one day after that. Everyone was so up, so energetic until we began to receive enemy fire jerking our aircraft into a different direction. Awaken moment! All five of us crew members grew up in the blink of an eye: "To Live or To Die for our Country!"

I quickly maneuvered the stick to lift the helicopter to a higher altitude. Good Lord! I was only 23 years old. I was pleased with my first safe and sound battle flight with my crew, but by the same token, I started becoming conscious of combat responsibility for my aircraft, and the needs of the fighting Marines on the ground. Again, the captain's voice was near, "Lieutenant Snyder, **I am the responsible person in charge of my own success.**"

During my 13-month combat tour in Vietnam, I flew 1,200 combat missions. I was shot down twice: once during the Battle of Khe Sanh in 1968, and once in Laos in 1969. I commanded all 24 CH-46s for all my missions, and zero was destroyed under my control. None of my comrades was killed or captured or left behind once onboard with me.

The Vietnam War marked the largest number of helicopters lost in any war. Total helicopters destroyed were 5,086 out of 11,827. Based on a database I got recently from the Pentagon, total helicopter pilots killed in the Vietnam War were 2,202, and total non-pilot crew members were 2,704. This really was the "Helicopters War!"

Fast forward to 1985, and I was appointed to work in the Pentagon during President Ronald Reagan's term. I was promoted to colonel while stationed there as well.

The most interesting thing was that I was one of the designers and funders for building the new SH-60 Seahawk helo. The entire team of 25 personnel spent two years in development, launching in late 1988.

The curiosity of a three-year-old farm boy was most fulfilled and satisfied. "Wow, I'm here in Pentagon living my dream of a pilot coming from the enthrallment of a three-year-old." The bond really exists, allied by the captain's voice, "**I am the responsible person in charge of my own success.**"

By the way, I made colonel after spending 20 years in the Corps. The good captain became Commandant of the Marine Corps 25 years later. He indeed was the uplift of his own destiny and mine too.

Still fascinating with flying, I became a commercial airline pilot after retiring from the Corps in 1991. I had a chance to fly many domestic flights from East Coast to West. Up in the air, I enjoyed viewing all the scenery down below; the oceans, ranches, forests, mountains, harbors, and city lights.

Somewhere in that scenery, especially over the ranches, I saw the icon of the three-year-old boy gazing up to my airplane windows. I'm flattered! I'm proud! I was living my life successfully and rewarded, both in my military career and the civilian world.

Seventy years later, from the three-year-old farm boy's obsession and the captain's voice, my half-a-century flying experience is accident-free, a wonderful journey, and a great blessing from Almighty God! So, to all my friends or whoever knows me, don't be surprised when you catch me somewhere on the street looking up at the sky reflecting the three-year-old farm boy's moment.

A Woman's Life in The Military
By Vernita Black

Military life is inspiring and exciting. When I first joined the military, I was anxious but ready for the new adventure. I was unsure of what to expect or how I would fit in; however, I was confident about beginning my journey into military life. I was always positive and gave 100 percent to whatever I faced, whether It was shining my shoes to a glass-like polish, putting crisp creases in my uniform, or making my bed with perfect hospital corners.

I always put my best effort into accomplishing the task ahead, regardless of its size, and regardless of the challenge, chaos, or other disappointments in my life. I would not allow myself to be destroyed by trials and tribulations, and when I faced a challenge in life, it usually made me stronger and better prepared for the future. Naturally, I also had to face struggles, pain, and disappointments and even serious, life-threatening events, which not surprisingly, usually seemed to be part of my military life.

I joined the Air Force Reserves in 1981, and I enjoyed it from the very beginning. Basic training was a different kind of experience for me since I had done some exercising and working out, but not to the same level as in the military.

Looking back, the adventure had begun on a positive note. I managed to get through the physical and mental parts of training, but a few years later, my attitude changed, and I wanted more from military life. The Air Force had been very good to me, and I learned many important skills with the experience. In the Air Force Reserves, the once a month schedule was not enough for me, and I wanted to serve full-time. I decided to go on active duty. As I mentioned earlier, I tend to keep moving forward in whatever situation I face.

I made a quick and intelligent decision about my career. I went to my supervisor, letting him know that I wanted to go on active duty with the Air Force. He looked into my request and replied that I could go on active duty, but not with the Air Force. I was shocked.

The Air Force had been great for me, but I had to follow certain rules to qualify for active duty. First of all, my age would disqualify me from active duty. Each branch of the military has their own requirements, and I had already reached the threshold age limit for the Air Force.

I was upset and felt devastated about the requirements, but I was also determined to pursue going into active duty. I had to consider the other military branches. This also meant that I would have to redo my basic training. I thought about it for some time and decided to go for it. I joined the United States Navy active military.

Was I happy about it? Absolutely not! But I knew that if I were to reach my dreams, I would have to stretch further. I even surprised myself when I signed the papers to go back to square one. It was my choice, and I was determined to be all right with it.

My friends and family thought that I had lost my mind, but I felt strongly that I was doing what was best for me. I wanted to be of service to my country and to feel good about myself. It seemed to be the best thing to do, and I wanted to make the most out of it. So, off I went back to basic training. Boot Camp! I had heard that Navy training was more difficult than the Air Force version, but I still made it through relatively easily.

To be honest, the words BOOT CAMP had always scared me. I had never been through any type of strenuous training except for my ballet and swimming in high school. Still, I thought that I was ready, and could face any challenge coming my way. When I left for basic training, I weighed 100 pounds and felt strong and ready to take it head-on.

I arrived in Orlando, Florida ready, willing, and able to move forward with this new adventure. I felt excited, happy, eager, and energetic to begin. Initially, when I arrived at boot camp, it felt like I was in heaven, but that changed when I was assigned my location. Orlando was beautiful and peaceful, but it changed dramatically after an hour. My life shifted so quickly that I thought I was in a new time zone. I became anxious and scared for the very first time.

My first encounter was with a drill sergeant. Within 15 minutes of arriving, I was called so many names that were nowhere on my birth certificate. I did so many push-ups in the first 30 minutes that I lost count. Actually, I think I may have broken my own record for the most push-ups. My mind wandered, my thoughts were racing, my body was in shock, and I only wanted out. There was no way I could put up with this mess, and I needed to find my way home as soon as possible.

Then I suddenly snapped to a different level of consciousness. I decided that I wanted to stay and face the challenge. I decided that I could do it and would not let them scare me away. I was resolved to stay focused, positive, and make the best of my situation.

I continued with the grueling challenge: the mind-blowing adventure. During the first couple of days, everything happened so fast; it was hard to keep up. Being older than my first time at boot camp, the challenges seemed different from those in the Air Force. I was up early every morning until late in the evening, preparing for the next day of agony and pain. I yearned for my home chores, which seemed so much easier than the ones I faced at this camp.

In the next eight weeks, I had to deal with many physical and mental challenges, with just enough time to take a few deep breaths and continue. Eventually, it got easier, more interesting, and even a little fun at times. I was ready to move forward with the next phase.

When basic training came to an end, I graduated again in the United States Navy. I was ready to proceed with more learning and training. I had always liked school and thought that this would be easy for me. I like math and learning new things and chose engineering and electronics, a field that has few women in it. My job involved fixing many kinds of communication systems and electrical and navigation systems throughout the ship. I was thrilled to be part of this department, though women in engineering often face challenges.

During my academic military training, I did very well, and I was in the top 10 percent of my class. I was proud of my accomplishments, and because I was near the top of my class, I could have my pick of a duty station. I was overjoyed to be stationed at Long Beach, California. What a beautiful place!

In my 21-year career in the military, I was assigned to various duty stations. My very first encounter with a navy ship was overwhelming, but with time I became more familiar with the operations. I was stationed aboard a tugboat, which was completely new to me. Being one of two women on the tugboat, I felt somewhat intimidated. Although I never felt comfortable, I was there to do my job.

In the 1990s, I was assigned to my first naval ship, the USS Cape Cod (AD-43), a destroyer tender. What a colossal ship! I was both excited and nervous and thought I would never find my way around the ship or fit in with the rest of the people. Eventually, I met the challenges, just as I had done in other situations. I learned a lot about the military, and again I felt I was ready to move on to something else.

After that assignment, I was stationed on shore duty for a while and then transferred to my first combat ship, the USS Kinkaid (DD-965). Women were limited to serving aboard certain kinds of ships and my new situation was kind of scary and different from being aboard a tender. During this time, I was part of the Desert Storm, Desert Shield operation, which was especially challenging as both men and women served aboard combat ships

My mission increased further when I was stationed aboard an aircraft carrier, the USS John C Stennis (CVN-74). This duty was more challenging than on any other vessel on which I served. It took a few weeks or more before I found my way around.

Despite the many challenges in serving active duty, I was always able to work them out. Although working in the U.S. Navy was only possible with teamwork, all kinds of adjustments were required. At the end of our mission, we had fulfilled our duties to protect and serve.

My ultimate goal was to serve our country. My tasks were not always easy or fair, but they always had a purpose to them. All men and women serving in the military have the same goal – to serve and protect – and they do so to a different degree. I am proud to have served in the finest military on earth, the United States Armed Forces.

Confirmed Last Transmission (Roger That)
By Thomas Calabrese

The mortars dropped in on the Marines like fire from hell, and the jungle warriors instinctively dived for cover. The screams of anguish of those who had been hit filled the morning air, and once the location of the enemy's mortar position was determined, grunts grabbed their weapons and raced into harm's way while corpsmen risked their lives to tend to the injured. Coordinates were radioed in and, medivac helicopters responded as controlled chaos encompassed the area. Grunts revved from zero to ninety in less than a second, their hearts pounding in their ears, blood pumping through their veins, and adrenalin fueling their muscles. Once the injured were taken away and the enemy was neutralized or escaped, the ground-pounders gradually downshifted from overdrive to neutral.

It was May 15, 1969, and the clear and search mission was in its forty-fifth day in the Quang Nam province of South Vietnam. Lima Company, Third Battalion, 26th Marines fought the entrenched elements of the 31st and 141st North Vietnamese regiments in Operation Oklahoma Hills.

There were hundreds of fighting Marines in the jungles of South Vietnam today, trying to be as precise and workmanlike as possible when calling in mortars, artillery, and air strikes so as not to kill their brothers in arms. Combat patrols were doing their best to stay within their sector of search, and they always radioed in before returning to their own lines, so as not to be killed by friendly fire.

The Marines of Lima Company were exhausted, but they humped on because stopping or giving up was not an option, nor was looking any farther than the next ridgeline or valley. They were in search of an elusive enemy who had burrowed deep into the ground and only came out of his hole to inflict death and injury.

Every time the Marines took a break, one could always be heard turning to his buddy and grumbling about the weather, the bugs, and even the roots of trees and plants that reached out to trip somebody in the column. The simpler the gripe, the more effective it was, for if a Marine had complained about the morality of war, it would have been too broad a subject for men who survived by keeping things as uncomplicated as possible.

A Marine infantryman travels by ankle express, but what helps him keep going is that he always has somebody or something to blame for his situation. Logically he knows that it doesn't do him a bit of good or change things, but it feels a whole lot better putting it out in the open than letting it eat him alive holding the festering frustration.

In Vietnam, most combat Marines didn't know what they needed to know until they had learned it firsthand, and hopefully when they did know it, they would still be alive for it to do them some good. When first platoon set up camp for the night in a 360-degree defensive position, the Marines used the remaining minutes of daylight for some personal time.

Corporal Johnson took his writing tablet out of a plastic bag and wrote a short letter to the folks back home. Nothing specific, just something to let them know that he was still alive.

PFC Dowell had a dog-eared western novel by Louis L'Amour, called *The First Fast Draw*, that had been passed around from Marine to Marine and he picked up reading where he had stopped the evening before.

Lance Corporal Rader had an old *Star and Stripes* newspaper, and even though most of the pages were too wet and crumpled to decipher, that didn't stop him from trying to read it.

Corporal Ciccio was browsing through a *Reader's Digest* magazine, focusing most of his attention on "Humor in Uniform" and "Word Power."

Sergeant Farmer was talking to Lieutenant Callan about the killer teams and the personnel assignments for the night ambushes, which included call signs and locations to set up the Claymore mines.

Many different types of communications happen during a normal day in the life of a Marine Corps infantryman and it is easy to overlook or take for granted how vitally important each one is for survival; as important as food, water, and ammunition. Communication can save the life of a Marine at one moment and in the very next one, it can touch his soul, bring a tear to his eye or whisk him away from a horrendous situation to a place of tranquility and serenity. The language of war and the military experience is colorful, innovative, brutal, and ironic.

The light of day faded away, and when the night came, it was like so many others before it, every sound played tricks on the Marines' imaginations until they thought the enemy was sneaking up on them from every direction and the cloak of total darkness took on human forms. When the sun filtered through the jungle canopy at sunrise, the Marines awakened with a sigh of relief that they were still breathing. Some began cooking their C-rations, others checked their weapon, and a few pulled out their novels.

For the next two weeks, the men of Lima Company did their duty, suffered their losses, and continued with their assigned mission. Nobody knew when Operation Oklahoma Hills was going to end, but everybody had a guess, which was based more on hope than on fact.

"You know what today is?" Ciccio asked as he took a swallow of water from his canteen and wiped his mouth with his dirty shirtsleeve.

"It seemed like we've been out here forever," Johnson answered. "Is it Christmas yet?"

"It's Memorial Day," Ciccio replied.

"How do we celebrate?" Dowell interjected.

"Nobody celebrates Memorial Day; it is when you go to the cemetery," Rader said.

"If I don't make it back to the world, are you guys going to come put a flag and flowers on my grave?" Sergeant Farmer asked.

"Where do you live?" Cassidy asked.

"Omaha, Nebraska."

"I'm in Salt Lake; can I just mail some plastic ones instead?"

"When I look down from heaven, I'll know who has been visiting me, and I'll put a good word in for you with the Big Guy upstairs," Sergeant Farmer promised.

"Really," Hanford said.

"I will," Farmer reiterated.

"I mean, do you really think a reprobate like you is going to heaven, you'll be lucky if they take you in hell," Hanford joked.

"In case you haven't noticed, we're already in hell," Farmer sighed.

Gunnery Sergeant Garcia, a seasoned veteran of the Korean War and two tours in 'Nam was listening to the conversation and walked over and advised, "You know how you celebrate Memorial Day when you're in combat?" When nobody answered, he continued, "You survive, that's what you do. You survive and do your duty. When a baseball player comes up to bat with the bases loaded, he doesn't hold up the game to do a tribute to Lou Gehrig and Babe Ruth or contemplate his Hall of Fame speech. You guys got enough to think about right now, comprende?"

"Roger that, Gunny," Williams responded for the group as the command to move out was passed down. There was no more talk of Memorial Day from the Marines because when Gunny Garcia said something, everybody paid attention.

Later that afternoon, First Platoon came over the ridgeline and was moving down the trail into the valley when they came under heavy fire from three sides. Bullets ripped through the jungle foliage as the Marines frantically tried to find anything that they could hide behind. The North Vietnamese were so well concealed that it was hard to identify their exact locations. The situation went from desperate to critical in less than ten seconds when mortars began hitting nearby. It wouldn't take long before the enemy gunners would make the necessary adjustments and start dropping the rounds directly on top of the Marines.

Just when all seemed lost, the sounds of jets approaching in the distance could be heard. They dropped their bombs with pinpoint accuracy on the ridgeline and then strafed the area with their 20-millimeter cannons until the enemy fire ceased.

Lt. Callan called out to his men, "Who called in those airstrikes?"

No one answered, so he demanded, "I repeat, who called in those airstrikes?"

Lance Corporal Beaumont, the radio operator walked over with the shattered, AN/PRC-25 radio and held it up for all to see, "It caught two rounds, it saved my life, but it was useless the whole time."

The broken radio crackled to life, and a clear voice was heard to say, "Confirmed last transmission. Glad we were able to help you out."

"Roger that," came the response from an unknown voice.

Lt. Callan looked around at his men, but he didn't have any answers for them, "If the radio is not working and nobody called in those strikes, does somebody want to tell me what we just heard, and who that was talking on a shot-to-pieces radio?"

Gunny Garcia pointed upward at the clear blue sky above the Marines and flashed a big smile, "Maybe some Marine didn't feel like being buried today."

On Memorial Day 1969, a profound and unexplained form of communication went to the top of the list.

The Two-and-a-Half Pound Mouse
By Charlie Wyatt

It is a truism that war is a grim and largely soul-destroying business. I would agree wholeheartedly with that. However, I'm also certain that from the Babylonians on, every conflict has prompted, at least for some of its participants, a smile from time to time. That was certainly true of my tour in Vietnam. I was in charge of a 50-foot Swift Boat—fast, but aluminum hulled and vulnerable.

In our quarters, the guy who had the bunk next to mine, Doug Thome, came back from liberty one night with a little creature in hand. To all outward appearances, it was just an average-sized brown mouse, weighing a few ounces. Doug had transported it in an old sneaker, with one of the laces around its neck as a kind of collar. I wasn't very impressed and said so, "What the heck do you want with that thing?"

"Well, he didn't cost much, 25 Piastres; less than a buck. I thought he was kind of cute, like a mascot, you know. And now I have somebody to talk to that's more intelligent than half the people around here."

The mouse was resting his forepaws on the edge of the sneaker and staring unblinkingly at me. I had to admit it was cute.

"What's his name?"

Doug said, "I tried calling him 'Twai,' which I think is Vietnamese for mouse, but you know how tricky that tonal inflection can be, so I dropped the idea. I thought I might call him Mickey, but that sounded pretty used up, trite. So, I settled on Ralph."

"Why Ralph, for God's sake?"

"I don't know. I have a cousin named Ralph, and this guy looks kind of like him."

"Okay, but don't expect me to look after him while you're on patrol."

"Certainly not. He's going on patrol <u>with</u> me."

And so, he did, in what would become his traveling home, that old sneaker. Ralph rode on the ledge inside the cabin, often half out of his shoe, gazing forward at wherever the boat was heading.

We were going through a bad patch right then, boats getting shot up, guys getting wounded. That meant all of us that could had to do 24 hours on, followed by in theory 18 off. As a practical matter, as soon as a boat came in, it was fueled, restocked with ammunition, and sent out again, meaning you were lucky to get 12 hours off. Surprisingly, during this time, Doug saw no action at all.

At the end of a week of that, Doug brought the 38 boat in, about half asleep by the time he reached the dock where I was already standing, ready to take over. The boat needed only topping off with fuel, and we were on our way. It wasn't until I was well out in the channel that I noticed Ralph still on the forward dashboard. I gave him a half wave by way of salute, made sure he had some of the seeds which he consumed at a great rate, and then forgot all about him.

We ran into no trouble at all that patrol, and when we returned, I carried Ralph back up to the barracks and reunited him with Doug. Two days later, Doug had another uneventful patrol. I was scheduled for Station Pumpkin the next night, way up the Soi Rap River, a place notorious for ambushes. As I was getting dressed, Doug looked over from his rack and said, "Wanna take Ralph along?"

I hesitated, then said, "Sure, why not."

We saw lots of tracers and chased a couple of phantom radar contacts, but ended up not firing a shot. After that, it was understood by Doug and me that whoever was out would take Ralph. Not that we talked about it, and we would have denied being superstitious, but hey, if it works, don't mess with it. We were sometimes shot at, but the difference between being shot at and being shot up, as anyone who has been there can tell you, is profound.

As time went by, the bad patch slacked off, we got fresh crews from the States, and things were generally much better. Meantime, Ralph went on a growth spurt. He couldn't fit in his sneaker at all and was promoted to a shoebox. Also, he now ate virtually anything and everything. When he hit roughly Guinea Pig size, he became impossible to take on patrol; there was no way to harness him, and he would run all over the boat. Besides, he seemed to feel somehow that his work as our resident rabbit's foot was done.

He now lived in a space between my bunk and Doug's where we each had a four-drawer dresser side by side but facing opposite ways. We fixed him a place between the two dressers in a wooden box, where he was content to remain, for the most part, eating—which he did a lot—or sleeping.

On a lark, one evening, Doug poured a little beer in a jar lid and Ralph slurped it up. After that, he seemed to think he was entitled to some anytime either of us had any. In addition, anything even remotely edible couldn't be left where he could get at it— soap, anything leather, care packages from home, all were fair game for our now oversized, almost spherical, mouse.

One day as we were speculating about how much he weighed, I had an idea. I talked the mess hall cook into giving us some ground hamburger. We then molded that into roughly Ralph's shape and size and weighed it on a scale, which for some reason was calibrated in kilograms. It came out a touch over a kilo.

"Wow," Doug commented. "Right at two and a half pounds."

Once we'd determined our mouse's mass, we began to theorize why the rodent had attained such a monstrous size. I said, "Maybe right at first, when you were trying to call him mouse in Vietnamese, the tonal inflection was off, and he thought you said moose." Or, "You know that high-intensity reading lamp you use. Maybe he spent too much time under it and somehow mutated. I mean, if it could happen to the Incredible Hulk, well, you know."

Doug, though, had the most reasonable explanation. "You know they've discovered a species of deer back in the mountains here that's no bigger than a good-sized cat. And how about those three kinds of sea snakes just identified that were unknown to science until now. Maybe Ralph belongs to a previously unknown giant mouse species."

Whatever the case, we were now short-timers, with less than 30 days left in our tour. The question was what to do with Ralph. Both of us were pretty sure that if we just left, our Vietnamese housekeeper would kill him, to say nothing of what the base commander would do if forced to take official notice of him.

In the end, two days before rotating out, we popped a cover over his box when he was sleeping and carried him some distance away from the base before setting him free. He was too fat to sit up on his haunches anymore, but as he crouched there staring at us, it was all I could do to walk away.

On the big transport winging its way over the Pacific, going the right direction this time, I thought about Ralph. In addition to serving as our good-luck charm, he had served to take my mind off the grueling and increasingly pointless war. Just caring for him and seeing him basically content amid chaos, boredom, and danger was a source of satisfaction. I hoped he would adapt to being free and on his own, and soon enough find some cute female, settle down, raise a family, and altogether thrive. It's wishful thinking here, but maybe Ralph was hoping the same thing for me.

Parris Island .... Yellow Footprints
By Leif K. Thorsten

They herded quickly, the Bulldogs did
Amid the yelling, the cursing, the chaotic din
The boys from the towns, the cities, and fields.
Down the Halls of Montezuma bare
And with determined minds, feet they placed
Upon the Yellow footprints there.

Gone the hair as clean as a shave
Then the civvies, the jewelry, all were replaced.
No photos of sweetie, nothing of home,
Remove the past only the present to share.
In boots that don't fit, the feet they placed
Upon the Yellow footprints there.

In shirts of white and trousers green
Crawling face in the mud, backs ripped by wire
They all look the same now, you see.
Climb 40-foot towers if only to scare
The daring young boys whose feet they placed
Upon the Yellow footprints there.

It's spit and polish for all must shine
It's yer left yer right, again and again.
To eat on the march and fall in line,
The rifles do crack; rounds split the hairs.
And the Marines have earned where their feet are placed
Upon those Yellow footprints there.

Now it's transition from this to the civilian scene
Upon stepping stones, the military provided,
To stand together among the proven
The people from all walks united.
Face adversity with confidence, place firmly your feet
Upon the Yellow Footprints of Life.

How to "Snap Roll" a SC-47 on Takeoff and Survive!
By Hal Sprogis

The B-36 and B-47 crews that had just scrambled aboard our SC-47 strategic rescue aircraft, together with our crew, were in for a BIG surprise! Our aircraft was moments away from having a catastrophic crash and the demise of all of us if it were not for *four* fortuitous events.

So, what is a snap roll anyway? It is an occurrence in which an aircraft experiences a loss of lift (a stall) with full or substantial engine power and as a result becomes uncontrollable and enters a spin. Normally spinning down vertically from a high altitude, like 10,000 feet, is routinely practiced with training aircraft and recovery is usually made at a lower, but safe altitude, such as 5,000 feet. Such a snap roll at 50 feet is *decidedly unwelcome*! After stalling, our aircraft entered a *horizontal* spin, rotating 90 degrees in about one-second, with the left wing nearly scraping the ground. That was the first fortuitous event when our wing *did not* plow into the ground avoiding an immediate crash!

That was not the total end of the drama. What had to be done now was completely counterintuitive! The power from both engines had to be CUT immediately to recover from the spin and hopefully be able to level the wings for a "controlled crash" into a grove of pine trees that lay ahead!

In a split second, I chopped the throttles, with the faith that aileron control would be regained, preventing the aircraft from continuing its roll into an inverted crash. This second fortuitous event was *decidedly welcome,* as the aircraft responded, and we achieved a roll back to a wings-level position. We now had only a few extra moments to savor our existence, since without power, only seconds remained until we would fatally strike the ground, the grove of pine trees, or both. We were still in a dangerous stall, or were we?

It was then that I noticed the airspeed indicator showed 65 knots and *increasing*! We must have come out of the stall, but how? Moments later, we understood our third fortuitous event and why we had flying speed. Upon takeoff, we had fired our JATO (jet assisted takeoff) bottles. They were attached underneath the fuselage to boost our takeoff power from the short 1,000-foot-long improvised landing strip, just south of the Iron Curtain.

Could we still regain normal flight if power was returned? Gingerly, I advanced power *without* the aircraft stalling and rolling onto its side again. Lucky for us with our fourth fortuitous event. We barely made it over the top of the pine trees.

We were happy!

Our crew was stunned by these events and remained speechless until we leveled in cruise at 100 feet above ground level. I then went back to the cabin to try to figure out what happened.

A colonel immediately said, "Captain, that was some takeoff you made back there!"

I did not know what to say. After a few moments, I spotted what might be the problem. Crews aboard the aircraft had been practicing escape and evasion tactics for several weeks and had brought with them hundreds of pounds of equipment that they used during their training. Instead of putting this weight onto special racks over the center of gravity, they had dropped all these items on the floor near the aft cargo door. A check of the weight and balance revealed that this caused the aircraft to be far out of limits and into the prohibited danger zone! A small oversight by the tactical development team but one that needed correction.

Our mission was to rescue downed crew members deep inside enemy territory in the event of nuclear war while staying clear of Soviet territory during these practice rescue operations. Later inflight refueling and newer aircraft made such operations unnecessary. Of course, now, missiles have replaced almost all aircraft as nuclear delivery systems.

This event so influenced my future in aviation, that after joining United Airlines in 1956, I withdrew from airline flying to work at Engineering Flight Test, resolving safety issues. After several years, I returned to airline flying and later earned the first Aviation Safety Certificate from the University of Southern California. Aviation accident investigation and safety service became a calling, as part of my 50-year piloting career.

Man Up or Get Posted!
By Calvin Coleman

Combat is extremely challenging for many service members. Facing the possibility of death daily is enough to overwhelm any human In the case of the combat zone that was the setting for the account that follows, add the element of an erratic, narcissistic commander.

February 2004 was a time when most Americans were beaming with pride because of our nation's successful campaign against Iraq. Thanks to its might and muscle, the United States military had overrun Saddam Hussein's forces in a very short time.

After America had captured Baghdad and President Bush had announced, "Mission accomplished," the Magnificent Bastards (2/4) were selected to provide stability and sustainment operations in Ramadi, Iraq. Following the invasion, the new mission was to provide security and stability, until the country could vote for government officials. The Magnificent Bastards is the nickname of the Second Battalion, Fourth Marines, Fifth Marine Regiment, First Marine Division. During this time, I served as the gunnery sergeant of Echo Company. The Echo Company commander was Captain John Appert.[1] Captain Appert was a stocky Caucasian man about 5' 10" tall, with dirty blond hair, blue eyes, and an ego from hell. I thought he was smart, but his authoritarian style of leadership was difficult to bear. He led with force and made sure there was no doubt that he was the man in charge. Captain Appert also was one of the most knowledgeable military tacticians that I have served with during my 20-year career. His lack of people skills and abrasive personality were his major shortcomings. Captain Appert's personality led the battalion commander to give him the call sign Porcupine Six.

He would challenge anyone, with an intent to win every conflict. I remember Captain Appert showing up at his change of command with a fresh black eye. The executive officer told me that

---

[1] Names have been changed to protect the privacy of individuals the author was deployed with.

Captain Appert had been drinking with officers of the battalion the night prior and had had a fight with another captain. Someone finally tried to put him in his place, but nothing changed.

One day, Captain Appert noticed the black belt around my waist. Wearing a black belt in the Marine Corps meant that I completed the martial arts course and was certified to teach Marine Corps martial arts. He glanced at my belt, gave me his typical steely-eyed look, and asked, "What the hell do you know about martial arts, Gunny? Aren't you a little too old to be rolling around with the young Marines?"

I was not sure how to respond, but I could feel my blood boiling with testosterone. I felt like he was purposefully questioning my ability in front of the junior Marines, in an attempt to discredit my accomplishment. I am sure his comments were meant to let the Marines know that he was the top dog. I tried to control my tone of voice and responded, "If you want to go out back and test my skills, you are more than welcome, sir."

He shrugged his shoulders and laughed, then gave me a snarly grin and walked away. Just as he was about to depart the room, he said, "You would be better off fighting Conan the Barbarian with a butter knife than mess with me. Gunny, you need to stay in your lane!" At this point, I knew it would be in my best interest to shut my mouth and drop the issue. This response was typical of Captain America, the name that the Marines of Echo used in private.

On February 20, 2004, Echo Company departed for Iraq, arriving on February 24. The company was sent to a city called Ar Ramadi, commonly referred to as Ramadi. While in Ramadi, each company of the battalion was assigned areas of coverage and lived in a forward base, called a combat outpost. Echo Company was located on the east side of the city, furthest away from the battalion command post. Our location was ideal for Captain Appert; it was far enough from headquarters that he was free to act however he chose without supervision.

Echo Company was provided an abandoned nuclear and biological training facility as our combat outpost. The outpost had large stone walls around the perimeter about twelve feet in height, providing decent cover from fire. The combat outpost also had a vehicle staging area with overhead protection, which was important because we received mortar fire daily.

Within the walls of the outpost were several abandoned buildings. Most had holes in the walls from previous mortar fire. We transformed the bullet-riddled buildings into living quarters. We worked nonstop to fortify the facility and make it defendable, an almost impossible task. The combat outpost looked like a small fortress dressed in concertina wire and green sandbags. Our new home had no bathrooms, no running water, and no electricity. Living in an environment with so little had a significant impact on the morale of the unit as time went on.

Somehow, Captain Appert found ways to make the almost unbearable living conditions a little better, but only for himself. His room always had an air conditioner and electricity because he had a gas-operated generator. One of his friends, a fellow officer that worked in supply, provided him with that generator. Almost every day, Captain Appert came out of his air-conditioned room and attempted to start a conversation with his Marines, usually bragging about his success in the military.

Prior to Captain Appert's assuming command, to have some idea of what to expect of my incoming commander, I asked one of my friends who worked in administration to conduct a service record review on him. I found out that he was a prior service enlisted airman who drove buses for the Air Force. After his first enlistment, he attended college and joined the Marine Corps as a commissioned officer. He also had no combat experience, and that really concerned me. I wondered what type of commander he would be when the bullets started to fly.

As the deployment went on, the unit lost trust and confidence in Captain Appert due to his erratic behavior. Most of the unit's members felt that he was trying to be a war hero and use the company like pieces on a chess board to be sacrificed. I attempted to focus on the mission and not our differences. However, the power struggle between him and me was not difficult to see.

Echo's previous commander had not deployed with us because he'd received orders to the East Coast a week before our deployment. Following his departure, I became the next-most-familiar person in the chain of command. When I told the Marines to perform a task, though, Captain Appert came right behind me and told them to disregard what I had said, flexing his muscle in an attempt to show who was in charge.

His behavior made the Marines of Echo hesitant to act without his approval. This loss of trust within the command placed a significant amount of stress on me. I once told my wife that combat was easy; dealing with my commander, not the enemy, was my struggle. At least when the enemy got out of line, I had courses of action I could take.

My daily routine was to conduct maintenance checks of the combat outpost and to stand watch in the command-and-control center, monitoring the activity of patrols and communicating with higher headquarters. The typical watch lasted 24 hours and was a day-on-day-off post. When not on post or engaging in maintenance of the post, I conducted security patrols whenever possible. Conducting patrols increased my bond with the Marines. However, I was in a constant state of fatigue due to this rigorous schedule. At one point, I resorted to placing a single piece of Copenhagen snuff in my eye; the burning sensation woke me up and enabled me to continue.

On May 12, Echo received the order to conduct a "cordon and knock" on a house. A cordon and knock is a military tactic used to surround a building before a forced entry occurs. Our intelligence claimed a high-value person was using the house as a hideout.

On that day, I had the command-and-control center watch, but I really wanted to be part of this special mission. I felt like my presence was needed. I coordinated with Lieutenant Wrobleski, the platoon commander who was my relief, and asked him to relieve me early. Lieutenant Wrobleski said he would relieve me early if his platoon returned to the base camp in time. As Lieutenant Wrobleski's platoon came through the gate, Captain Appert radioed and requested to exit friendly lines. I granted permission to exit, ran out the gate, and jumped in the last vehicle. I threw my gear in the vehicle and told the driver to give me the radio, via which I notified the first sergeant to add one more to his count and informed him where I was.

The convoy continued to exit the gate slowly. Once the last vehicle exited the gate, our speed increased. The dust kicked up by the convoy floated like a tan cloud, leaving an indication of where it had been. The convoy gained speed until less than a quarter mile out the gate a large explosion took place.

The fog of war descended upon us. Dust, debris, and darkness were everywhere! All of the vehicles pulled to the side of the road, hoping to identify the person who triggered the explosion. Once my vehicle stopped, I jumped out with my full combat load, which weighed about 170 pounds and included a flak jacket with protective plates, helmet, and eight full magazine pouches. I also had three weapons: an M4 service rifle, a M249 squad automatic weapon, and an M9 pistol.

I ran in a mad sprint to investigate the damage. Upon arriving at the Humvee that had been damaged, I assessed the situation. I observed that the vehicle was stuck in a crater, with the rear of the vehicle still on the road. The front end of the Humvee had been swallowed by the crater; all I could see were the tail lights. All the same, on this day, we were lucky. The trigger man had initiated the improvised explosive device (IED) too soon, and no lives were lost.

Once I figured out that all were safe, I developed a plan to recover the vehicle. I grabbed a radio and yelled, "Platoon Sergeants, I need four or five of your largest Marines, right fucking now." I planned to use the weight of the large Marines as leverage on the rear of the Humvee, to gain enough traction for the vehicle driver to back out of the crater. I instructed the Marines to stand on the rear of the Humvee, and then I told the driver to place the vehicle in reverse. We needed a little more weight, so I joined the burly men. As we stood on the rear of the vehicle, jumping, the vehicle finally started to gain traction.

Just as the vehicle began to back out of the crater, Captain Appert arrived. He marched up to me and said, "Gunny, get your ass off that damn Hummer." He then asked, "How many vehicles do we have out here?"

I replied, "Sir, I have no idea, but I can't talk right now because I got to get this fucking vehicle out before we start receiving fire."

Captain Appert retorted, "How in the hell do you claim to be a company gunny if you don't know how many vehicles left the fucking outpost?" I wanted to explain, but not just then. My primary concern was to free the vehicle and carry on with the mission because often insurgents would follow an IED explosion with some sort of direct fire. Because I disregarded his order, Captain Appert cursed me out in front of God, country, and corps! Then he grabbed my leg and said, "Get your ass off the vehicle and go and count my vehicles."

I jumped off the vehicle. Once my feet hit the ground, I placed my face inches from his. I screamed in my best Drill Instructor voice, "I am tired of your shit, and so are the Marines of Echo! You can un-fuck your own damn vehicle! I am sick of this bullshit! I am going to get the hell out of here before I do something that I fucking regret!"

I stormed away, heading towards the combat outpost. As I began walking down Route Michigan, a route commonly referred to as IED Alley, the Marines in the convoy stared at me in disbelief.

When I arrived at the combat outpost's gate, the sentries yelled, "Halt who goes there!"

I said, "It's me, Gunny Coleman, shut up and open the fucking gate!"

One of the sentries yelled, "Advance to be recognized." Once they realized it was me, they asked me why I was alone and if I was ok. I told them I was fine and that our convoy had been hit and that everyone was ok. I immediately went to the command-and-control center to provide a status update on the convoy.

Once I provided the briefing, I went to the vehicle staging area and sat in an empty vehicle. I needed time to gather my thoughts and prepare myself for what was about to happen to my career. I wondered if this would be my last day as the company gunnery sergeant. Was my act enough to take my rank? Moments later, I heard the roar of a convoy entering the main entrance of the outpost. It was Captain Appert returning to base. He must have realized that the element of surprise was lost.

About an hour later, the first sergeant found me. "Gunny, I need to talk to you about the incident that took place." He told me that I have the right to remain silent and that anything I say can and would be held against me in a trial by court-martial. He proceeded to read my rights and asked if I wanted to talk.

I told him that I was sick of Captain Appert's attitude and that I couldn't take his nonsense anymore. After I made that statement, I decided it best to keep my mouth shut. He told me to hit the rack and we could talk in the morning. I walked to my room wondering, "How do I talk to a lawyer in a combat situation?"

The following morning, the executive officer came to my room. He arrived with a piece of paper in his hands. He read my rights again and asked me if I wanted to talk. I told him there was no need for me to talk because I might incriminate myself.

He laid the paper on a desk and asked me to read it. The paper was a non-punitive letter of caution. It stated what I had done and that my behavior was not acceptable. It listed several corrective measures that I was to take if I planned to continue as the company gunnery sergeant. I signed the document, and about 15 minutes later, Captain Appert entered my room without knocking. He counselled me on my conduct and his expectations. I bit my tongue as he spoke. As it turned out, the non-punitive letter given me that morning was the first of three that I received on that deployment.

August finally arrived, and I was selected to be part of the advance party. The advance party returns home ahead of the main company to prepare for the arrival of the rest of the company. I conducted one final mission that day and then caught a helicopter to Al Assad, an airport made by the coalition forces. Prior to boarding my plane, I called my wife to let her know that I was on my way home.

About two days later my plane landed at March Air Force Base, Riverside, California. As we debarked, we were given a hero's welcome. The first thing I did was call my wife. All I said was, I made it! My wife told me that she had spoken to the first sergeant's wife earlier and that she had informed my wife that Captain Appert had been relieved of his duties as company commander. The executive officer was now the commanding officer.

I was shocked but happy at the same time. The higher headquarter had decided to conduct a climate survey to assess how combat had affected our unit. The climate survey revealed Captain Appert's attitude, and it was determined that he was not fit to lead due to loss of trust and confidence. It was gratifying to learn that, even in an organization as large as the United States Marine Corps, the system can work and do the right thing.

The Case of the Lilac Toilet Paper
By Lawrence J. Klumas

The Air Force teaches leadership under actual work-related conditions. The Air Force makes a point of placing its young officers in situations where they must learn to exercise judgment and maturity. In so doing, the military creates its own leaders from within. Those young officers who learn fast, get promoted. Those who don't, don't. This principle is fairly simple.

What is not necessarily simple are the situations in which young officers must call upon their wits to make instant decisions and live with the consequences of those decisions. The challenges cannot be anticipated. Sometimes young officers' quick decisions work for them, sometimes against them. Accumulation of experience gained in decision-making situations creates better, wiser leaders.

The process described above is illustrated by one experience I had as a new First Lieutenant in the 92nd Civil Engineering Squadron at Fairchild Air Force Base (AFB) near Spokane, Washington, in October 1966.

Arriving at Fairchild was an eye opener. The South-East Asia (SEA) Vietnam conflict was ramping up, and many of the Air Force Civil Engineer Officers (those assigned to Base Civil Engineering units) were being deployed. As it turned out, because of these SEA assignments, with just under two years of professional career experience, I ended up as the most senior Engineering Officer on staff. This was a little scary.

in September 1966, Fairchild AFB was tasked as the Strategic Air Command base to sponsor Bombing Competition (Bomb Comp). It was an important test of bomber crew training. It was also a prestigious event, requiring an enormous amount of planning and preparation by the host base to guarantee the six-day event merited all the hype it received.

During the 1966 Bomb Comp, one crew and one aircraft from the 35 separate B-52 (Stratofortress) wings and 2 B-58 (Hustler) wings were to compete. In addition, as a spectator's delight, Britain's Royal Air Force had three crews, flying the Vulcan bomber, scheduled to participate.

It was a huge production for the host base to ensure all the operational planning went flawlessly. This included planning for the incremental scheduling of aircraft for on-time takeoff, night celestial navigation, two low-altitude bombing runs (four releases), and one high-altitude bombing run (two releases), as well as the scoring units' dispersal throughout the Western Fly Zone to record the simulated bomb drops.

Just as important was the logistics support for Bomb Comp; to allow the crews' maximum concentration on completion, logistics had to be seamless. This was accomplished this by tasking the host base organization with countless details in support of the overall effort.

For Civil Engineering (CE), the CE project manager and I had to see to it that numerous tasks were developed, tested, implemented, and tested a second time, and relatedly, task all the craftsmen and professionals to make sure everything worked. It was my responsibility to confirm that the power grid was tested, the runways were swept, the grounds were immaculately manicured, and the highly polished fire department engines were always in place at the right time. In short, and above all, no glitches, Lieutenant!

Of course, it took mountains of ribbon, posters, rope, stations, and barriers to channel all the activity in the right directions. One of the special features was the lilac toilet paper placed in all the proper locations, in honor of Spokane being the Lilac City. No plain white toilet paper, no sir – lilac toilet paper.

The crews and their spectacular bombers were to arrive on Monday. On the Friday before, Lieutenant Colonel Ratto, the overall base project officer, called me at 0700 hours. He said, "The Base Commander, Colonel Roderick Patton, wants to see you right now."

"What for?"

"To make sure everything is in order in the Civil Engineering camp, Lieutenant."

Panic began to set in. I hurriedly called our supply order desk, for the sticking point was, the lilac toilet paper had not arrived as of last night.

"Sergeant, is the toilet paper here yet?"

"No sweat, Lieutenant. It is due here at 7:30 am sharp!"

Armed with that assurance, I proceeded to the Base Commander's office. After I had waited a few minutes, his executive officer, smiling, said, "You can go in there now, Lieutenant."

I reported.

"How is everything going, Lieutenant?" Colonel Patton spoke calmly. It was unnerving.

"Fine," I said, but with a lump in my throat. And everything was all right, except for that damned lilac toilet paper. The time was 0755 hours.

"Good, good, good," he said, and looking up at me, tilted back in his chair. "You know what, though. I am a little worried about that lilac toilet paper coming in on time. Are you?"

I mustered all the courage I had and pronounced, "Yes, sir, it arrived at 0730 hours this morning." I was sweating. I wanted to sound positive, but somehow my words echoed inside my head as if I were speaking into a 55-gallon drum.

"Know what? I am going to call the supply Sergeant, right now, and ask him if the toilet paper is here--actually, physically here. And if it is, that is great. If it isn't, you weren't telling me the truth."

The blood was pounding in my ears. Heavy thumping sounds. I felt a cold white ashen pallor creep over my skin. But I thought out what I had to do instantly, and responded, "No sir, do not call. I did not go there and see for myself. I need to do that. With your permission, I will do it right now and be back in ten minutes."

"Good," he said. "I like that answer. See you in ten minutes."

I arrived at the supply point at 0822 hours. A supply truck was backing into the loading dock. I hopped up and talked to the driver. The five pallets of lilac toilet paper were in the truck, and would be off loaded momentarily. I waited for the first pallet to roll into the supply room.

Ever feel relief? I did. In fact, I was elated. Why? Because if I had not admitted my mistake, admitted to it on the spot to the Base Commander, my military career path may have taken a turn into a totally different future.

And I learned a valuable lesson, one that has stayed with me through my military career and into all the other career jobs I have had in life. This is the lesson: For critical Issues, do not take the word of another. Go and see for yourself.

I did check it out, then, and thereafter. And to this day, I thank Colonel Roderick Patton, Base Commander, for allowing me to learn that very important lesson. Go see for yourself. Then you can speak with authority.

Duty Calls

By Eileen-Gayle Coleman

No matter where you are stationed in the world, "duty" is one of the things most Marines dislike during their time in active-duty status. Duty requires two or three Marines to stand a full 24-hour shift while the others work a regular 8-hour shift. Afterwards, they can go home, lay their cheeks on their cool, velvet pillows, and enter the shadowy world of dreams.

When I was at boot camp, it was a different story. Duty, which was called Firewatch, usually took place after hours when all the female recruits were in bed. We had multiple posts during the late night, and we were put on a very strict schedule that gave us very little to no sleep. Like a car, we were always close to running on empty. Waking up was no longer pleasurable. Sleep was the sole bit of freedom we had, a moment when we would all feel whole, only to be punctured when the screams of Drill Instructors began to pollute the air with rage and tension. Though we understood the purpose Firewatch served, not many of us understood the reasons behind it until one day, duty finally called.

For me, boot camp took place about four years ago in Marine Corps Recruit Depot Parris Island, South Carolina. The blistering cold of spring was finally ending, only to bring the fires of hell called summer to the small island that was my home for those few months. One night, the scribe informed me that I had Firewatch between the hours of midnight and 3 AM. It was one of the worst shifts to be assigned, because it was a struggle to get some sleep before it was your turn to stand watch. Shortly before midnight, I dragged myself out of the comfort of my bed into the night I had been dreading for the previous few sleepless hours. Once I took my post, I sat in an enormous semi-lit room, so I could look in at the darkened surroundings and all the recruits who were fast asleep dreaming about home.

The first couple hours lazily crept by, until I noticed one of the girls get up from bed. She tilted her head to me to indicate she was headed to the bathroom, and then disappeared behind the black flippy doors. I didn't think too much of it as I jotted it down in the logbook—"Rt Braggs entered the head at 0130"—then signed my initials next to the notation. Afterwards, I let my back lean up against my seat, rocking it back and forth as I stared up at the pale grey ceiling, counting down the minutes until my shift would end. I don't remember how long it took me to notice, but when I never heard the doors open with a clank, I knew I had to go see if Braggs was alright, or if she had just fallen asleep at the toilet.

Moving away from the desk, I headed toward the doors, opening them wide enough for my voice to enter the room. Her name echoed throughout the bathroom over and over until it faded away with the darkness. Then her agonized scream tore through me like a shard of glass. I felt my eyes widen and pulse quicken; my heart thudded like a rock rattling in a box. The scream came again, desperate, tormented, and before I knew it, my legs sped toward the distressed voice of Braggs. She sat rocking in the corner of an open stall, her eyes bloodshot with tears, her arms wrapped around her waist. Another one of the girls came rushing in. No doubt, she had heard Braggs' cry, as well. "What's wrong?" she asked frantically.

"I don't know. I just suddenly felt this pain," Braggs said, trying to hold back another painful scream.

"Where does it hurt?" I interjected.

"On my side and around my stomach," Braggs answered.

"Can you describe it?" I asked.

"I don't know. Sharp?" She sounded a bit irritated with that last question.

The other girl suggested that it might be a cramp, and to wait for it to pass. I felt differently. I've had cramps before, and they can be very painful, like a pounding migraine, but the way Braggs looked, it seemed like something else.

"Maybe I should tell the Drill Instructor?" I suggested.

"If you think so." Braggs barely breathed, her face turning pale as a ghost. It was hard to tell if she was terrified at the thought of an infuriated Drill Instructor being awakened from her sleep like a rabid bear, or if the pain from her side was worsening with every breath she took. The other recruit tried to comfort Braggs as I paced back and forth between the stall and the door to the Drill Instructors' hut. My mind raced between fear at the Drill Instructor's rage and concern at Braggs' crying in pain. The pressure was on. I could feel my heart trying to leap out of my chest as if to escape the anxiety I was feeling.

"Whatever you plan to do, please do it," Braggs whimpered.

With those words, I made up my mind, and ran towards the Drill Instructor's door like I was running into battle. I pounded on the door so hard that my hand went numb. The seconds felt like hours as I waited at the door. When it finally opened, I tried to calm my mind long enough to speak coherently so that the Drill Instructor could get a clear idea of the situation at hand. All the same, my words still came out in a rush, garbled. After telling me to shut up, she marched toward the stall where Braggs sat, still sobbing in pain. At first, the Drill Instructor had the look of a bomb, ready to explode, but like a light switch, her demeanor changed. Concern was now written all over her face just like ours, although she still had a bitter tone in her voice when she told us to scram.

I couldn't sit down. I wandered the floor, acting as if I was doing something relevant to my post when I was really wondering if Braggs was okay. I watched quietly as the Drill Instructor raced back and forth between her office and bathroom, a sense of urgency with every step she took. About eight minutes later, the sounds of sirens from a distance grew louder and louder until the flashing lights were outside the cement walls to our barracks, spilling into our bay. A few of the girls woke up to the commotion, and started asking questions as they saw Braggs being rolled out on a gurney. I honestly didn't know what to tell them.

Moments later, the Drill Instructor called me up and told me to write down everything that happened, in the logbook; she then left with Braggs in the ambulance. I listened to the sirens as they wailed down the empty street of Parris Island until all that was heard was the silence of the night. As I wrote, a thought came to mind, words that frightened me every time I saw an ambulance pass by: "When the lights and sound turn off, that means they lost the person inside that vehicle." I dismissed the thought, telling myself that Braggs would be alright and back later that day, but she wasn't. It was two days before she was finally released from the hospital.

The night Braggs returned, when we were given our free

time, we all went to her bed to hear her story, and what really happened that night.

"My appendix blew," she said.

We all had that deer-in-front-of-headlights look plastered on our faces. The girls started catapulting questions at her, wanting to know every detail, right down to the last time she pooped. After she answered every question, she went to find me. I was near my bunk, drawing a comic to put up on our motivational table.

Her words caught me by surprise. "Thank you."

"For what?" I looked puzzled.

"If it wasn't for you making that quick decision and the Drill Instructor calling the ambulance in time, I probably wouldn't be here."

I replied, "No need to thank me. I'm just glad you're alive." Every word was the honest truth. When I signed the papers to join the United States Marine Corps, it was for just such moments. I became a Marine because I wanted the chance to defend this country, and protect everyone I love in it. In choosing this path, I took inspiration from the words of Ronald Reagan: "Some people spend an entire lifetime wondering if they made a difference in the world. But, the Marines don't have that problem." Braggs' words made clear that, even though I was just a fresh recruit in boot camp, I had already "made a difference in the world."

The Rainbow War
By Leif K. Thorsten

Destroy all the foliage,
That was the plan;
The government called it
Operation Ranch Hand.

Spray the hills and valleys
With toxic herbicides.
Eliminate the bushes
Where Charlie might hide.

Though the *Colors* of our war
Could not be seen,
The deadly agents
Were *White* and *Blue* and *Green*.

We polluted the land
Where the troops were sent,
Laced it with *Purple* and *Pink*
And that *Orange* agent.

For over a decade
We sprayed all the plants;
It got in our hair, on our skin,
All over our pants.

No reason to worry,
That's what we were told,
So, we brought it back home
Where it slowly took hold.

The toxins ran deep
Where the blood did flow.
It spared but a few,
How were we to know?

A *Rainbow* of *Colors*
Slowly kills us each day;
Where Charlie had failed,
The agents lay us in our graves.

The Wife of a Military Man
By Shirley Turner

As the wife of a military man (Navy, enlisted), I had to learn many things. Some were very important—for example, one must be on time--and some relatively unimportant—for example, In the Navy, the bathroom is called the "head."

We married at an early age, both of us under twenty, so the odds were that we would have problems. The salary of a seaman is not a great deal of money, by any standard. Budgeting was the first lesson. The man of the house stood extra watches for cash. In order to save money, eating out became a very rare luxury. This necessitated my learning another lesson, how to cook.

With moves to different military bases, making new friends, and setting up apartments came several more lessons. I learned one must pack and unpack efficiently, and even then, precious things may be lost. I learned people are generally kind, and each new move taught me about both the different climates here in the United States and the many accents to be found in English. During this time, I also learned you must back up your partner, and you must be able to count on each other, always.

All of the aforementioned are important, but in the realm of life lessons, they are the easy ones. Life's college-level classes were yet to come. Sea duty for the man of the house required my assuming all the responsibilities normally held by him. Car maintenance, security, and nurturing a love for Daddy became a necessity. He was not at home, but he must not be forgotten. No internet or cell phones, so letters became life lines. Daily notes promised were written at bedtime: preschoolers' hand prints, sticks of gum, and reassurances that we would be waiting, no matter the length of the cruise, went out in the daily mail. But graduate school classes were on their way.

Vietnam required my Petty Officer 2nd Class to sail again, in a far more serious state of mind. The devotion, the home, and the three children we hoped to nurture—indeed, our entire future--was tenuous. Daily letters arrived once a week, in bunches. The evening news was a necessity. The support all the wives gave to each other was the lifeline for survival on the home front.

The life lessons learned during a military career involve the entire family. They are valuable survival lessons for business, personal encounters, and educational endeavors. Any college or graduate school education is expensive. After a marriage to a twenty-year career Navy man, I feel I have a PhD in life adjustment.

Tales of a Grunt's Battered Battle Boots
By Johnny Olson

While working on an advertisement campaign, I was asked to bring in some Marine Corps memorabilia for a photoshoot. One of those items was my beat-up Gulf War boots. I hadn't seen those boots in about 20 years. When I unboxed them, they prompted a stream of memories I'd forgotten all about. Hence the following story, which goes out to all my fellow Gulf War Veterans, but especially those of Dragon Platoon Weapons Company 1st Battalion 7th Marine (1/7). Semper Fidelis!

If these well-worn, war-torn, sand-beaten, sad-looking field boots had a voice, oh, the tales they would tell of scenes they had seen when they once enveloped this grunt's feet.

As I pulled the battered boots from an old forgotten box of Marine Corps mementoes that I was sifting through, this duo spoke to me and presented the keys to memories long ago locked up and put away. They came in rapid-fire succession; I replayed scenes that we, me and my old field boots, experienced during our time together.

In August of 1990 I was 19; I thought I'd seen my share in my years and knew what it meant to be a Marine. I even considered myself an "old salt," what with my 16 months in the Fleet Marine Force. In fact, I was just as pristine as my new boots. But me and my boots were about to be put to the test and pushed to our limits. We ultimately returned from it all, a bit war-torn and very well worn.

When we first bonded, my boots looked nothing like they did the day they retired from my feet, when the 7th Marines made our final escape from the sandbox in 1991. They were brand spanking new olive drab jungle boots that hardly matched the crisp and clean battle dress uniforms (desert cammies) they issued us Marines the day before we departed for Saudi Arabia. I'm not sure whether they were issued before or after we filled out our living wills, or got us a new batch of exotic experimental vaccines, or quickly studied our enemies' strategies and preferred means for defeating and deleting us infidels. But I digress.

When 1/7 landed in the Saudi Gulf, we were greeted by a wall of insane heat and intense humidity. It truly was the hellhole we were warned it would be. We touched down at the international airport, quickly loaded onto cattle cars, and whisked away to the port to unload ships containing everything a regiment of Marines needed to prevent a million-man Iraqi Army from crossing the Kuwait-Saudi Arabia border.

Marines have built a reputation for fighting fiercely and winning, despite the odds. The warriors of the "First Team" would not let our beloved Corps down by losing a battle, even if the odds were 1,500 to 1,000,000. We just needed to make sure we had an ample amount of ammo (check), a week's supply of MREs (check), and the rightly tightened boots upon our feet (check and check). Two dog tags were taped together so they wouldn't clink, with a third one tongue tucked and carefully laced up close to my feet in case I got blown up. Yep; chew on that one for a minute.

We left the port and trekked many miles through desolate desert scenes, patrolling for the sake of killing time and staying sharp. We got filled to the gills with sand along the way, caked with it until we got us some "rear with the gear" relief every month or so, when the Suck (Marine Corps) would deem us fit for a flattened mattress, a real shower, hot chow, and a shoddy layer of boot polish to keep the brass off our asses. We killed our share of shitbugs, trapping them in the front sole of our toe, whacking the other boot against it, and splat! shitbug no more. We got blasted with sand; our weathered skin was worn thin, revealing the tenderness within. We sat for countless hours playing Spades and Hearts and reading letters and writing back. We impatiently waited for something to happen that would ultimately get us back home. We swallowed our fears when the word finally came that the Shield had become a Storm. We wrote what we thought might be our last letters to our loved ones. We awoke in the middle of that last night, loaded up predawn, and crossed over the border into an unknown fate.

We saw nightmare scenes of blackened landscapes charred with oil and blood, disfigured bodies of melted enemies whose pedal to the metal wasn't fast enough to outrun the fury from above. We donned our gas masks and protective gear when the call of "Gas! Gas! Gas!" came down the line. We stormed the airport and stole back the country's only city, through orchard battles with their toughest troops. We warmly welcomed Kuwaitis as they crossed our defense lines to give us hugs and their country's colors. We were told to stop right there, that we did our jobs, and Saddam would live to see another day. We were slow-shuffled back Stateside and welcomed home as heroes by our nation's citizens, who had a heaping pile of stinking guilt from that jungle war that came before. Yep, me and my boots, we were mighty proud to have served. We did what we were designed to do when the time came to prove our worth.

I'm not saying that the things me and my field boots did and saw were as sad and horrendous as what other warriors and their battle boots endured before and after me. As we know, the Gulf War resulted in the swiftest victory our country has ever seen--and on our televisions, yet. But it was the scenes they didn't show on headline newsfeeds that most bonded this grunt with those well-worn, war-torn, sand-beaten, sad-looking field boots.

To some who were not there, these boots may look ready for the trash heap. To me, they are a reminder of a time and place that me and my feet never want to forget.

Take Away
By Kevin T. Byrne

My term of service was from 1970 through 1973 as an enlisted soldier in the U.S. Army. These were challenging times, not only for the military, but for society in general. Our war in Vietnam was a failure, but our warriors never failed. The men and women who served during the Vietnam era did their jobs and more; the politicians did not. What we took away from the experience, the good and the bad, defined our lives.

I was a Private First Class when one day, I was called into the Sergeant First Class' office and was told I was going to be responsible for the section to which I was currently assigned. The previous section leader, a Sergeant E-5, was being discharged. I thought about that for a minute, and then reminded my superior that everyone in the section outranked me, and it would create friction with the other guys. I suggested that I be promoted to Specialist 4th Class so as not to offend anyone. He told me I didn't have enough time in service, but he would talk to the Commanding Officer (CO) about the situation and for me to get started. This was long before the days of *Star Wars*, but the military concept that "resistance was futile" had already been ingrained in my bones.

When I informed my co-workers, everyone got a good laugh, and I had a sneaking suspicion the joke was on me. Besides my normal workload, I now had the responsibility for the work product and was accountable to the CO. The CO instructed me in no uncertain terms that quality and quantity of production went hand-in-hand, and both were inadequate in our section. Congratulations, I was promoted to Specialist 4th Class.

My strategy was just to keep plugging away at the work, improve my own work product, and keep my head low, which is difficult when you're "in charge." After about a year of this, the previously mentioned Sergeant First Class informed me of an opening for Non-Commissioned Officer (NCO) School for which I was eligible, and told me no one else in the unit wanted to attend. Sorely in need of a change of scenery, I quickly volunteered to enroll, once again getting a good laugh from my co-workers.

I spent twelve weeks in Indiana studying squad and

platoon level infantry tactics. Even though the war in Vietnam was essentially finished, the Soviet Union still posed a threat to Western Europe, and our Division was on first call to respond. I was a lowly clerk, but nonetheless, we could quickly be thrown into combat operations. The training gave us the tools needed to protect ourselves and function as a unit.

Along with field tactics, we studied the Army's 11 principles of leadership. These principles were published from lessons learned in World War II. When I returned to the "real world" and began my career, I discovered the leadership principles that I learned in NCO school were as true in the business sector as they were in the military. Without even realizing it, I integrated and then adapted those principles to my work, and found success doing so.

I've listed those 11 principles below. They stand as true today as when they were developed seventy years ago.

Leadership Principles
Know yourself and seek self-improvement.
Be technically and tactically proficient.
Seek responsibility and take responsibility for your actions.
Set the example.
Know your people and look out for their welfare.
Keep your people informed.
Ensure the task is understood, supervised, and accomplished.
Develop a sense of responsibility among your people.
Train your people as a team.
Make sound and timely decisions.
Employ your work unit in accordance with its capabilities.

Three Poems
By Lawrence J. Klumas

New Year's Eve on the Mississippi

Alone young airman stationed at Kessler Air Force Base
Mississippi wanted that special experience --
New Year's Eve on a Paddlewheel riverboat.
Booked and went.

Pretty teenage girl with jet-black hair
From Lafayette, LA wanting celebration with friends,
Dutifully tagged along with family,
Seriously doubting it would be enjoyable.

Sounds of the paddlewheel.
Lapping of the river on the keel.
Buzzing of couples in hushed tones.
Bursting wide open raucous laughter.

Dixieland band orchestra of note.
Loud, brassy happy songs.
Mysteriously -- next a welcome string
Of softer clarinet solo sounds.

The lone airman spotted
The solitary teen at the upper deck rail
Slim, short hair, mature features.
His request for a dance accepted.

They glided in quiet solitude, thinking.
Suddenly at their second dance -- a reversal,
Animated conversation, standing still, unconcerned,
Reaching one another's desperation.

Intimate beginnings, happiness looming
Within each one, no longer alone.
Shared needs discovered, telephone numbers
Exchanged, prospects innumerable glowing.

Follow on phone call Airman to Teenager,
Mother answered, stern words, berating!
Daughter is fifteen. No disreputable military
Man allowed to date her. Don't call again.

Rusty Nail

We were in the Officers Club,
        such as it was, of the
RED HORSE squadron compound
        at Phan Rang Air Base,
Late, after the 21:00 debriefing
        between the workers at the
Squadron and the Headquarters wienies.
The facility was newly renovated
        from an old French billet.
Sandbags were stacked up against the outside walls.
PSP (pierced steel planking) served
        as the welcoming mat
        at the entrance.
We could feel the rumble of the B-52's
        from the carpet bombing
        through the ground
Striking at the Ho Chi Minh trail,
        long before we heard
The stuttering airborne explosions
        miles away.
We talked of the same old things:
        the war (it could be won),
        sports (too many teams, too far away),
        girls (too few),
        sex (... right!),
        work (the real substance),
The real meaning for being there – construction!
        It's successes. It's woes. It's dog days.
        A few bright spots – completed projects.
Drinking Single Malt Scotch Whiskey and Drambuie.
One. Two. A few more.
So-o smooth, three parts scotch to one-part liqueur.
I stood up.
        My head spun.
I passed out.
           (... God save us all...)

Tail Gunners Viewpoint

Stuck behind the thick plastic shield,
Wedged in with parachute,
Little space to exercise cramped muscles
The tail gunner's world revolved around:
        The mission planner's target selection,
        The enemy's detection of his aircraft,
        The evasive maneuvers of the pilot,
        The power of the 50-cal. machine gun,
        The armament maintenance quality control.

Will his agilities work perfectly this go around?
        His training to remain calm,
        His eyesight to detect enemy aircraft early,
        His muscles to remain limber,
        His visual tracking abilities,
        His lead-the-target techniques,
Will he acquire and score first?
If not, his chances wane.

But he cannot think about this.
He must make every small individual thought,
Movement, and action count.

He must overcome the paralyzing fear of
Being shot inside his noisy vulnerable cubicle
With no joy of anticipation.

He must win.
They must lose.

Bend Me, Shape Me
By Garry G. Garretson

I look back on my days in the U.S. Navy, flying as an air crewman. We flew throughout Vietnam and Southeast Asia transporting troops, weapons, and other cargo. For my first eighteen months, we were tracking typhoons all over the Pacific Ocean or flying early warning for our Seventh Fleet off the Vietnamese coast. I had the privilege of flying as a radioman in C-118, C-130 and EC-121 aircraft. I can associate many things I learned that made a big difference in my performance during my forty years with a Fortune 500 Company.

After completing boot camp at Great Lakes, Illinois in January 1966, I had orders to electronics training "A school" and radioman training "C school" in Millington, Tennessee. The 36 weeks of intense classroom study prepared me to be an electronics technician and an inflight communications operator. We learned equipment repair, military voice communication protocol, and CW (continuous wave or Morse code) use.

My first fleet duty after graduation was with VW-1, Airborne Early Warning Squadron One, home-based at Naval Air Station, Agana, Guam - well known as the Typhoon Trackers. As I was a very junior enlisted man, I spent the first sixty days in "compartment cleaning," or housekeeping service for my fellow enlisted members. I then had TDY (temporary duty) orders for three months of repairing radio and navigation equipment in Chu Lai, Vietnam, with our Detachment "C," supporting our aircraft as they performed their duties in the Tonkin Gulf.

Before my time under the TDY orders to Chu Lai was completed, I was assigned as an Aircrewman, Second Radioman on the WC-121N- Super Constellation, a four-engine propeller-driven aircraft. My duties were then to keep all navigation and communication equipment operative, to transmit all high frequency (HF) communications and to keep records of all communication to and from the aircraft. Our overall duties were tracking typhoons throughout the Pacific Ocean, flying early warning for the U. S. Navy's Seventh Fleet in the Tonkin Gulf, off the coast of Vietnam, providing radio relay services throughout the theater of operation for TACAMO (ballistic-missile submarines) and training all others who were flying the "Super Connie."

After several deployments from Guam to Chu Lai, Vietnam as a Second Radioman, on Crew 9 and the first day of our third deployment, we were scheduled to fly our "routine" early warning patrol, which would last over fifteen hours. The First Radioman and I were completing the preflight inspection, around 1500. Just before the doors were to be closed, Mac announced, "I am really sick. You are on your own." I was nervous, but, First Class Petty Officer McMullen was one of the best trainers and gave me great confidence in my abilities to get the job done.

It took about an hour flight to arrive on Yankee Station. We leveled off at our cruising altitude of 4500 feet, ready to patrol the hostile area between South Vietnam, North Vietnam and the Chinese island of Hainan. The seventeenth parallel was the dividing line between the two Vietnams. I always felt we were between a rock, a hard place and, a time bomb. Some suggested we were the decoys that would provide early warning but that we were only sitting ducks. We had the aircraft carrier group to protect us, especially "Red Crown," the guided missile destroyer, and a massive number of intercept jets. Our guardians were impressive if it were assumed that they would be able to act fast enough, if we detected the bogies and relayed the information quickly. We would be flying at around 350 knots, but the Russian-built MIG's could fly at 1500 Knots and maneuver like eagles. Then there were surface to air missiles (SAM's) around Hanoi, that were a threat if we got too close to Haiphong Harbor.

Once leveled off, I immediately got a call from the aircraft commander informing me that, "My darn UHF radio is not working. It needs to be fixed ASAP." I quickly checked the black box and exchanged it with one of the other eight transceivers. Just a quick fix until the real problem could be identified, on a test bench, once we were back on the ground.

I was stopped by the navigator who said, "My LORAN (Long Range Navigation) tracking system is offline. We cannot track in this weather without it. Let me know immediately when it is fixed." I immediately pulled the box and found a blown fuse, replaced it, and kept checking to make sure that it did not blow again. I notified Ensign O'Toole, "Got it fixed, sir, you do not have to use the stars for tracking now." He laughed.

After several other minor issues had been fixed, I stopped in the galley for a cup of coffee. The Crew Chief, Chief Williams, was having a quick cup of java. He said, "How's it going, Garretson?" I responded, "Under control, Chief."

I was immediately informed that the intercom system for the eight users on the scopes, CIC (Combat Information Center) operators, was inoperative. I did some troubleshooting and found a loose wire, soldered it, and returned to my cold coffee - but not long enough to drink the entire cup. The constant problems with the electronics equipment were the worst I had ever encountered. They did not stop for the next ten hours, and I was sleepy, totally exhausted, and wondering just what would happen next.

On the intercom, I heard First Class Petty Officer Stevens say, "We are tracking a bogie, flying an intercept pattern at Mach 2

coming off the coast from Haiphong Harbor" (We tracked all air or surface movement, with special focus on any craft that did not respond to our IFF (identification friend or foe transmission.) "Maybe it's one of ours flying an unauthorized intercept practice run, or it could be a Russian MIG-19 with missiles and other weapons." He was half kidding, I hoped.

I listened on the VHF emergency channel, 156.8 MHz, as Commander Wright engaged the transceiver, "Red Crown, Red Crown, this is Rainproof 7. We have a bogie flying an intercept pattern. What are you going to do, over?" The response was, "We will wait and ensure that it is not a friendly, over." Lt. Commander Wright responded, "If he is one of ours and is that dumb to not respond to IFF, he deserves to be shot down. We have a crew of 15 on board. We are descending as low as possible. Do something fast, over."

There was no response. We were hoping to see a missile from Red Crown blow him out of the sky or an F-4 Phantom intercept the idiot.

We descended quickly to below 1000 feet, while our F-4 Phantoms could be seen on the scopes, flying an intercept for us - but not before we had it reinforced on the scopes. A four-engine propeller-driven "Connie," capable of 350 knots, being chased by a supersonic jet capable of over 1500 knots. The bogie would reach us before the F-4's would reach him. But where was Red Crown? Still waiting for President Johnson or Secretary McNamara to authorize the response?

Apparently, we had spotted surface movement earlier and had followed it too close to North Vietnam, which was what had sent up the MIG. We were sitting ducks for the MIG if he wanted to shoot us down. My mind was twirling, thinking about the danger of the continuing dive of the aircraft with 15 Aircrewmen on the "Connie," with the pilot determined to put it in the water if the MIG kept coming, knowing that not many would survive a water crash, with the big reflector on the belly, which would probably break the fuselage into pieces, but knowing that no one would survive if we were shot down. I could see the water below, and then I had a visual on the bogie pilot through the window over the port window, where my duty station was. He seemed to be just playing or seeing if our planes would respond quickly enough. I am not sure, but I thought I saw a red USSR sickle and hammer on the side. He found out that our fleet was too cautious as if they were still waiting for direction from the White House.

Finally, at below 500 feet and still descending, one of the CIC Operators announced, "The bogie is turning toward Hanoi." All the crewmen yelled in relief. The aircraft commander, Lt. Commander Wright, was visibly upset that the F-4's had waited to intercept and asked me to keep absolutely accurate records of the conversations, for later investigation. (As the in-flight communications operator, I had access to every transceiver and had the responsibility of keeping flight logs up to date and turning them in upon landing.) I made sure that my flight records were complete and ready for review, with every conversation from our aircraft and exact times.

After we left Yankee Station, I was summoned to the flight deck by the aircraft commander. He handed me a slip of paper that I was sure was my orders to a captain's mast or some other discipline, due to the constant problems with "my" equipment. The walk up the aisle of the airplane seemed to take forever. He handed me a list of some of the problems we had encountered and the fixes, signed by First Radioman McMullen. It had all been a set up to see how I would respond to problems under intense pressure (except that the MIG intercept was very real and not under the control of the U.S. Navy). I received a call on our high-frequency (HF) transceiver from "Mac" telling me that I was being promoted to First Radioman immediately. At first, I did not understand, but then it hit me that Mac was a NATOPS (Naval Air Training Operating Procedures Standardization) evaluator and that I was being tested over the whole flight, with only a few from the crew in on the plot.

The last hour flying back to Chu Lai was just fun, with the various crew members congratulating me and talking about missing me when I would be reassigned to another crew. We had flown over fifteen combat support flights together and had partied in Japan, Taiwan, Thailand, the Philippines and many islands throughout the Pacific Ocean as we tracked typhoons. It was a bitter-sweet time.

I was sad to leave Crew 9 but happy to be the First Radioman on Crew 7. I knew many of them, and the crew chief, First Class Petty Officer McKinney, was one of my golfing buddies. We also became a very tight-knit crew and flew into typhoons with over 175 knots of winds, flew over 15 additional combat missions together, had many liberty calls throughout the Pacific Ocean theatre of operations.

The trip through hell prepared me to become a NATOPS evaluator for radioman promotions, and later to teach radio school in the Navy to many other flight crew members. It showed me that I could handle pressure, respond professionally, and get the job done when it all depended on me. Fifteen crew members depended on me for communication and navigation when visibility was zero in a typhoon or when we were landing in blizzard conditions on Adak, Alaska, and the ability to communicate saved lives of those we served and of those on board.

In combat, while we were on the ground in Nam, we learned when to keep our heads down, along with the rest of our bodies, when to retreat and when to re-group; when to attack and when to move forward vigorously; and when to just sit, survey, and wait while we developed a strategy. All of those are valuable lessons to apply to a business organization or to be an entrepreneur, intrapreneur, socialpreneur, or another "neur" on our own or to making a big contribution under the direction of others.

Our veterans walk away with an accelerated learning curve, a devotion to integrity, a learned skill of diversity and inclusion in action, a demonstration of efficient performance under pressure, a learned value of accountability, a global outlook, an awareness of health and safety protocols (both for themselves and the welfare of others), technological savvy, sincerity, trustworthiness, personal maturity, endurance, stamina, and flexibility. They also may have overcome personal disabilities through strength and determination.

I later worked for forty years with a Fortune 500 company that provided contract management services that utilized my military experiences in custodial services, electronic repair, and maintenance of facilities. We served hospitals, universities, businesses, industries and public schools. My memories of military life surface as I compare service in corporate finance, HR, sales and organizational leadership. The foundation was laid, the desire to succeed was implanted, and the perseverance to implement critical missions became hard-wired. We learned to build on strength, to be the answer, to take full accountability, to develop others, to know the mission, and to complete the objectives along the way - regardless of dangers, fears, or circumstances.

Four Poems
By Bud Parson

Warhorse

There was an old Warhorse who'd been hit in the side,
The enemy was closing in on him, but he took it in stride.

Oh, there was no doubt, when you looked at his face,
You could tell, real quickly, he was way off his pace.

It is not very often that you will see,
A great old Warhorse down on one knee.

His strength seemed diminished from many hard years:
The battles, the victories, and the echoing cheers.

So, for whatever reason, he stumbled and fell!
We all gathered 'round to help him get well.

It was not our fault; we did not have a clue.
How do you treat invincibility? What do you do?

At first, we were staggered, by a sense of impending loss.
Warhorse kept hobbling on. "A rolling stone gathers no moss."

Time's a great healer if you're young and strong!
But not when you've battled ten lifetimes long.

So, Warhorse, it's time...drop your armor and your gear.
Just rest well, we all love you, there are no enemies here.

Our Patch: 1-9
Tribute to 2nd Platoon, Bravo Company, 1st Battalion,
9th Regiment, 3rd Marine Division, 1966-67

There are days I wonder, "Why them and not me?"
Because I've had another 24 hours on my lucky living spree.

Still can't get to sleep at night just thinking of them.
Get up, do the perimeter sweep and forget about the REM.

How is it that I came back from all those terrors?
Oh yes, I was young, a "greenie," and I made some errors.

Now I look back and say, "I did my best."
I did my job well and, plus that, I even passed the test!

That's right, I ran through the bullets, hoping to survive,
To come back from each battle with all "my guys" alive!

And I made it to the last day of Operation Deckhouse Five,
Everyone got hit in that battle but, they all came out alive.

Of all that got shot I was taken up first.
They said I'd patched everyone up even though I was the worst.

I never saw "my guys" again, they just "choppered" me away.
Did any survive? A four-day coma and I don't know to this day.

I think of that battle often, and I'm still easily consumed,
By the fact that, for some reason, I knew they were doomed!

Plagued by this notion through so many sleepless years,
And the very thought of my being alive brings on my tears.

They were my family, albeit, for a very short time.
We partied together; drank: nickel beers; shots for a dime!

I would go back into battle, today, with those guys, if I could.
This time I would make sure the results would be better than good.

Everyone would come back without even a scratch.
And for our bravery, we would earn a brand-new battle-patch.

So, whether a guy survived, by luck or by using his head,
His Patch would commemorate the fallen men of 1-9...The Walking
Dead.

A Band of Brothers

This band of brothers came from everywhere.
It was formed, "in country," while we were there.
For those of you that have never been,
You'll never know the hell we were in!

The things that we saw; the things that we did.
The memories we see; the ones that we hid!
Unless you were there, you don't have a clue.
You think we've changed and we don't trust you.

When we went to war, we were so stinkin' young.
We came back, and no victory songs were sung.
The country that sent us, left us for dead.
Yet, one at a time, we found each other, instead.

We started vet groups; men poured in like a flood.
We called each other "brother" with no link by blood.
All our blood was left on the ground in "our" war!
We opened our arms to each other; you slammed the door.

Yes, now we have this huge band of brothers; it's us!
There are those in this country, who wonder, why fuss?
Weren't these the same ones who talked down the war?
While we laid down our young lives like never before?

Only God knows our sacrifice when we went to fight.
He still hears our screams from terrors of the night.
He knows we're changed; so different from the others,
So, He keeps us close, so that we can be; A Band of Brothers.

Jungle Blood

Time stopped for me in Vietnam, in a pool of my own blood.
I remember lying as flat as I could, the ground, like red mud.
The fragments of grenades being lobbed into our position
Were hitting my helmet and flak vest with scary precision.

I don't know why there was a swell of relief washing over me,
I hadn't been shot the eye; from that, I had come away free.
There was still the premonition of being shot in the left arm.
That had come to be; I was bleeding out, much to my alarm!

The radioman lay face-down and quiet; communication out.
My radio-savvy was, but most would call, "in doubt."
I flipped over, crawled to him, keyed the mic., it squawked.
I didn't remember the radio codes, I just held down and talked.

Still had mic. in hand, could barely see, but, I could sure hear.
The sound of the choppers I had summoned were very near.
Found out later my time on the radio was heard at main base.
Who got to us first, helos or 2nd Platoon? Some called it a race!

2nd Platoon ran up as the first chopper landed in a clearing.
I could only see a paisley pattern, but I still had my hearing.
Then they laid down a ton of cover fire and rescue started.
Noisy boots running towards me zig-zagging as they darted.

A voice asked me if I could stand and I felt a helping hand.
I was up in a moment, on my way to life off this bloody land.
That was my blood I left behind, where so many left theirs.
Do you think it nurtured the jungle floor or maybe no one cares?

Between the Lines
By Glen Foss

The year was 1968, and the submarine on which I served as Weapons Officer had just returned to San Diego from a seven-month Western Pacific cruise. The return trip had been marked by a shortage of officers due to promotions and transfers, as well as by a change of command that took place at our brief stop in Pearl Harbor. The new Commanding Officer (CO) had an urgency to establish himself and ran training drills and exercises constantly, even though we were returning to a long period in port. The crew was tired and just wanted to get home, so morale throughout the ship had declined during the transit from Hawaii. I found myself in a billet that was customarily held by an officer a full grade senior to my rank while still trying to catch up on my submarine qualifications. The position of Weapons Officer included that of First Lieutenant, meaning that I was responsible for the maintenance of the ship's exterior.

Life with the new CO did not improve that much after our return to San Diego. He had a style that was unpredictable and grating, and both officer and enlisted personnel became the recipients of his wrath.

Our homecoming berth was at the Anti-Submarine Warfare base near the Naval Training Station. Our boat had won the squadron award for battle efficiency the previous year, and we proudly displayed a large white "E" on our sail. It was a new year, however, and the battle efficiency title was going to another sub. The day after our arrival in San Diego, the Executive Officer (XO) gave me instructions from the Captain that I needed to get the E painted over. No details of timing were given. My leading seaman (submarines did not have bosun's mates) informed me that we had no paint on board and that we would have to send someone to the 32nd Street Naval Station to procure paint. I knew that we were scheduled to move to Broadway Pier the following day, which was much closer to the naval station. Because we were short-handed and the trip to 32nd Street would have tied up two or three men for half a day, I opted to wait and do the painting the following day when it would take less time to secure the paint.

The next morning, as we were preparing to get under way for our move, I was called into the XO's stateroom, where I received a stern lecture. The Captain had not been pleased when he arrived at the ship and found the battle efficiency E still on display. I was informed that it was professionally embarrassing for the Captain because we were no longer authorized to show the E.

A few days later, I was duty officer when the Captain left the ship in mid-afternoon. He left his copy of the Union-Tribune and told me to save it, because he would return in the evening for it. He did not return that evening. The next morning, when the steward was preparing the wardroom for breakfast, he asked what he should do with the paper. (Note that the wardroom on a diesel submarine is about the size of a civilian middle manager's desk, and a newspaper takes up the seat of one officer.) I told him that it was the Captain's, that he had not come back for it the previous evening as he had said he would, and that it would be OK to throw it away. As you may have guessed, the Captain arrived shortly thereafter, and I was taken to the woodshed again.

The incidents above were more the result of my immaturity as an officer than of any fault of the CO, though his behavior later became an issue. My failure to read between the lines on those and several other decisions in my brief military career highlighted my lack of preparedness for a leadership position and an ignorance of organizational politics. I tended to get into trouble for what seemed common-sense actions to me. I had grown up on a farm, where I had learned to recognize work to be done and to do it. There was no one to supervise, to influence, or, with the exception of my father, to please. In college, I had learned, among other things, how to study, take notes, perform on exams, and drink beer. Students learned leadership skills through participating in student government or being president of a fraternity or other organization. That did not apply to me, but the Navy recruiter had been convincing when he told me that a college degree prepared me to be an officer. The sixteen busy weeks of Officer Candidate School provided little more than the basics of Navy life for future officers. Submarine school taught us how to operate and survive on submarines.

I would like to be able to say that the above lessons

enabled me to avoid such missteps in my subsequent civilian career. They did not—completely—but they did help to sensitize me to some third rails. I had learned to respect much about the way the military organization got things done. I found later that things as basic as an appreciation of the roles of responsibility and authority tend to be lost on civilian managers, who usually think, mistakenly, that they have more efficient ways of getting things done and holding people accountable. I also learned that it is not good leadership.to create a culture in which workers, be they military or civilian, are afraid to do their jobs

My brief military career also provided me with some non-academic lessons in psychology. I learned that, when boundaries are relaxed, personality and behavioral quirks are magnified. Maritime law, as well as Navy policy, endows the commanding officer of a vessel at sea with virtually unlimited power. That has proved the undoing of Naval and Merchant Marine officers through history, and the CO noted above was one of them. He had great skills, but his unstable behavior and poor treatment of his crew earned him a letter of censure, relief from command, and banishment to the recesses of the Pentagon—but not before the careers of several of his subordinates had been damaged.

I have witnessed similar phenomena in civilian life. The power of a manager over the lives of his employees tends to be much less absolute than that of a ship's captain, but the military example has provided me with insights into office politics. Neutrality in organizational power struggles is usually the best policy, but it is not always easy to achieve and can be seen as disloyalty by both sides. Reading between the lines may not be enough; reading comprehension is key.

For the Rest of My Life
By Ron Pickett

June in Florida is hot, and muggy and buggy. Pensacola is in the panhandle, and people sometimes refer to it as south Alabama.

It had not been a good week for me, in that June of 1956. I had failed to run the obstacle course in the qualifying time, and when the test results came out for Celestial Navigation, I had failed! What made it worse was that it was the final week of Navy Pre-Flight School. The next week, my sixty fellow company members would go to Naval Auxiliary Air Station, Whiting Field to begin primary flight training without me.

In truth, flying for the Navy was not something that I had always aspired to do; it was not a lifelong dream. I was offered the opportunity while I was going through boot camp in San Diego as a Seaman Recruit. I had enlisted in the Navy for two years because— well, you know—I was tired of school, wanted to see some of the world, and the other excuses that infuse the brain of a late-stage adolescent male. Boot camp had been fun, and I excelled. I was told that I was qualified for several officer candidate programs. I said, "Which one starts first?" They said, "The Naval Aviation Cadet Program, NAVCAD." I said, "Sign me up." My test scores were high on the aviation suitability tests, and I did well on the flight physical, so, why not?

Pre-flight was a good experience; the athletics—wrestling, gymnastics, boxing, and other contact sports, with lots of swimming (it is the Navy after all) and the famous Dilbert Dunker, the ditching trainer, it is aviation after all. The classes were interesting—meteorology, aerodynamics, power plants, military leadership, navigation and code Morse code, ah, that got a lot of people). Then there was the obstacle course; it was laid out with the usual obstacles—a barrier, a wall, things to jump over, and the deep, ever-present sand to drag you down. Over the sixteen weeks, my time improved, and at the end, I was only a few seconds shy of getting under the time limit. I would have one more try! Celestial navigation entailed finding stars, then looking them up in a book and reading the numbers. Except there was one little thing that somehow, I missed—Interpolation. If you know what it is, fine;

if you don't, don't worry. It really doesn't matter; it did then though.

So, come the next Monday morning, I had a room to myself and two more weeks in Pensacola. That had to have been the low point in my short life. Earlier I mentioned that I was not one of the people who did everything possible to fly for the navy. One of my High school buddies was one. I don't know whatever happened to him—but I didn't see him in Pensacola.

It's obvious that you don't want people being trained to fly military aircraft who don't want to do it, so getting out is easy; it's called DOR, Dropped on Request. It's staying in that's hard. But, after sixteen weeks, I had become quite strongly committed to that foolishness. They do a lot of things to make the Gold Wings seem like the most desirable object in the known and probably the unknown universe.

However, the double whammy of two failures to overcome and seeing my classmates pack and leave made it a very long, emotional weekend and one that was filled with questioning, self-doubt, and flashes of DORing. I could be out of the Navy in a little over a year and with the GI Bill to help in getting a degree. But there was something inside me that said, "Bullshit, (although I don't think that word had become an ingrained part of my vocabulary yet) you aren't a quitter. You can do this, and you are going to do it."

I think it was on my third flight with an instructor that we watched a T34 crash and burn off the end of the runway as we were preparing for takeoff. That caused me some second thoughts about my resolve.

Fifteen years after I retired from the Navy I ran across a woman who had worked for me. She told me that she was applying for a graduate program, and, in response to a requirement to write about someone who had a major influence on her life, had written about me. She said, "You expected more from us than we thought we could do, and we did it!" That style may have come, in part, from my experience at the end of preflight forty years earlier.

But, I did learn a lot about myself from that event that has been helpful for the rest of my life, for the 26 years in the Navy, and in civilian jobs following retirement. I'm tougher than I sometimes think, I don't have to follow the crowd and do things in lock step, I often take a different road, I'm free to experiment, I look for opportunities, I stay positive, and I could add a bunch of other clichés about darkest before the dawn and others—but that's enough.

So, whenever I'm down, discouraged, or depressed, I return to that long weekend in Pensacola in the hot summer of 1956, smile, and get on with it.

And, it's true that there were times when hurling my soft and tender body at the back end of an aircraft carrier in the middle of the night made me wonder about how smart that decision had been. Since I'm telling this story, I suppose it was smart enough.

Oh, you may ask, how much did I use Celestial Navigation in the ensuing 26 years of flying? Except to identify an occasional star on a clear night on the beach, never.

Woman Marine (never forget it)
By Shara French

Firearm; copper colored cartridge case. Pointy green-tipped brass bullets. Glittering ammunition. Smooth cherry-wood butt stock and dove-gray painted gun metal. Big barreled jeweled weapon. Marine's treasure. High powered rifle donned Marine. Machine gun, ammo tote en' mama. Peace, protection or propaganda? Symbols or honor? A woman Marine. Remember it. Never forget it. You are a Marine warrior

goddess.

Appearance; be modest. Keep neat and attractive, always. A feminine hair style. Hair will not fall below the collar's lower edge. No adornment. Nails one quarter inch long, or less, from fingertip edge. No fancy froo-froo nail polish. Nix loop-de-loop fobs and baubles. Zero gaudy chokers or bangles. Limited jewels. One ring per hand, only. Tattoos okay. No gang affiliations. Bright red or purple lips forbidden. Think scantily clad, make-up

appliqué.

Headgear; cover is a hat. Stop sign shaped top hat. Eight razor creased points atop. Decal ironed on hat front is eagle, globe and anchor emblem. Black emblem embedded, imprinted in your forehead like a brand. Crown hat or clown hat? Black Marine Corps emblem, symbolic, iconic, amniotic. Hypnotic. A brotherhood. Marine's Hymn. Memorize all three verses. Forget? Black-ball punishment. Semper Fidelis, Latin for always faithful. Marine Corps

Motto.

Wear camouflaged green hues and beige-blotched brown material. Must be pressed. Sharp ironed knife edge creases down fronts and backs of jacket arms and pant legs. Soak camouflaged uniform in starch and cold water. Hang and stiff dry in hot sun. Press HARD straight down pant leg center. Re-iron inside-out along same crease. Repeat. Right pocket centered sewn Nametags. Tiny tin black kiwi wax can. Spit-shine black leather boots. Spit shine your boots to mirror reflection, Marines," Sergeant Major said. "See your teeth in the boot toe." Twist cloth on index finger. Spit at toe. Make small black wax circles. Twist, spit, polish, repeat. Buff end-less-ly. Buff beau-ti-fully. Buff to gleaming glory. Boot shine reflects pride and sparkling

teeth.

Mission; stand ready to serve God, Country and Corps. Hiking with 70 lbs of gear and shooting and war-training. Alice-pack precisely packed: extra cammie uniforms, green socks, t-shirts and skivvies, extra cover, hygiene gear, sleeping bag, rubber bitch. Must have your mini shovel called an E-tool. Aweek supply MRE's (Meal-Ready-Eat). Fill portable stove bag with water to heat. Lean bag on rock to get hot. Insert plastic food pouch. Give it about five minutes. Now you are good to go! Sergeant said, "DO NOT forget your

shit paper.

Marching; orderly group movement; march in a formation stepping together. Four rows of thirteen men in each squad. A platoon formation. Each man, each step, same foot. March as one.

"Center yourself!"

Align head and shoulders squarely with the head and shoulders to the man to your front. Listen to commands. Immediately react to yelled cadence. Or get black-balled. The Marine platoon leader shouts and screams out cadence. Ditty commands used as each step is marked with the words, *"left, right, left..."* setting a march rhythm. Listen to the rhythm as fifty-two sets of feet pound...the...ground. *"Left, right, left, right, left. When I say left, your left foot strikes the deck. Left, right, left, right, left."*

Pristine; M-16 rifles are oiled and cleaned in religious ritual-like motions. A clean weapon assures a faithful bullet's hit. Accuracy is life or death. Love surrounds a Marine's weapon. They have pink haunting names like Marilyn Monroe or Anna Nicole Smith. A Marine sleeps with his M-16A2, lightweight, semi-automatic, air-cooled rifle with a maximum effective range of 550 meters. Compulsively thinking, rubbing, shooting and loving their weapon. Borderline

obsession.

What I Learned in The Military That Helped Me Later in Life: Go to Church
By Richard Meyer

When you join the military, you don't know what the future will be. When I joined, I felt I was about average and would be an average soldier. You must leave your family and friends when you join the military. It's easy to make friends because others are in the same situation. A little boy on a train said one time, "I know how to make friends...be friendly."

During basic training, you are kept too busy to have friends. After you have arrived at your unit is when you start making friends.

The chaplains and the chapels on base were a big help to me and prayer. I was surprised how much religion was provided in the service, love, and obedience towards God. I would have thought it would be less emphasized. Even when you are in the field, the chaplains are there having services on the hood of their jeep.

At home, I went to church, but I always had my family to help and support me. In the Army, I had to rely on religion and prayer to help me, which I continued after I was discharged.

At Ft. Ord where I had basic training for eight weeks, you were now allowed to leave the base except one weekend when they had an open house for your family. I went to San Luis Obispo where my cousin Stan was a pastor and had a nice visit with him and the rest of my family. I had one cousin, Eddie who was killed in WWII as an Army pilot, so you don't know what might happen to you when you are in the service.   My brother Andy was in the Army in Korea during the Korean War and returned home safely.

In basic training, they had a signup sheet for a religious retreat for a weekend. I wanted to sign up but did not. Another time they asked if anyone would like to sign up to be a Chaplain's Assistant, I wanted to sign up but did not. I began to think what was I doing, that I was going in the wrong direction.

I went to chapel on Sundays during basic training and met

some friends I went to high school with, Dave I met also went to Ft. Lewis, Washington when I was sent there after training.

At Ft Lewis I was in the M.P.'s and I felt a lot of pressure on me and, this is when I prayed hard for God to help me and He helped me do my job and finish the Army successfully.

After the Army I started a welding shop with my brother Jack and through prayer, going to church and working at the church, I had a successful business

Wing and A Prayer

The 1944 movie that devastated the Japanese Naval High Command

By Frank Ritter

This story was related to me by my then father-in-law, Robert Fennell, and his brother, Col. Paul Fennell, USMC (Ret.).

During World War II, Robert Fennell was a vice president of 20th Century Fox Studio and was the liaison between the Fox Studio and the War Department in Washington. At the same time, Col. Paul Fennell was assigned to Naval Intelligence. He was an animator who was interviewing US naval commanders after the battles of the Coral Sea and Midway and turning out animated recreations of the battles that the Navy used for training purposes. He did that all through the war, and, after the war, he interviewed Japanese commanders for their sides of the battles.

Soon after America's major defeat of the Japanese navy at the Battle of Midway in July 1942, Bob Fennell was approached by an admiral in the War Department. The admiral handed Bob an outline for a movie that the Navy wanted Fox to make immediately. It was the story of Carrier X. Bob was told that it was how our fleet wound up being where it was at the beginning of the Battle of Midway and that the public had a right to know how we had done it. He added that the Navy would supply all the military equipment that would be needed. Bob did not know that the US Navy had, in fact, broken the Japanese naval codes and desperately needed to hide that fact. The movie was the Navy's solution to that problem.

Fox Studio immediately set to work. They attached three of their major stars, Don Ameche, Dana Andrews, and Charles Bickford, to the project, which was to be directed by Fox's top director, Henry Hathaway.

The studio then did what all studios do best; they created an illusion that both mesmerized and enthralled audiences the world over—Including the Japanese naval High Command.

After the war, Col. Paul Fennell was interviewing high-ranking Japanese naval officers who let slip that when they had seen that movie, they had convinced themselves that they had already lost the war. They knew that America only had four combat-ready carriers at the beginning of the war. They erroneously believed they had sunk the USS Yorktown during the Battle of Coral Sea earlier in 1942. However, the Yorktown had been repaired in time for it to fight in the Battle of Midway, where it was sunk.

The Japanese High Command believed they had sunk two of America's four carriers . . . and then they saw the movie: That movie had known and recognizable actors in real TBF Avengers, Dauntless Dive Bombers, and Grumman F4F Wildcat fighters on what was quite obviously the flight deck of an aircraft carrier at sea. They closely examined everything in that movie in minute detail. They paid special attention to the pilots' ready room. They were looking for flaws that would tell them this was not a real ready room—and not a real carrier.

They were stunned. It was a real carrier!

How could they ever win a war against a country that has lost two of its four carriers and yet takes one of its two remaining carriers off the line to film a movie? How could they ever win against such certainty, such bravado? They came to the conclusion that, by mid-1944, they had already lost the war. They didn't stop fighting, but they had given up winning.

The Japanese naval high command never bothered to ask their own movie people how they would have made such a movie. They simply assumed that America had pulled a carrier off the line to make the movie. After all, there were shots from a distance of aircraft taking off and landing on a carrier at sea and even some launching and landing shots from the carrier's tower—all stock shots from prior movies that had been edited in for realism.

Even if the Japanese high command had figured out the stock shots, the diamond centerpiece of the movie was the carrier itself.

Fox Studio had built a complete, full-sized carrier flight deck, including the operations-bridge tower, six feet off the ground on their back lot (which is now the location of Century City, CA).

The aircraft, from the Los Alamitos Naval Air Station near Long Beach, CA, were flown into Santa Monica, CA's airport and then taxied down Pico Boulevard to the studio. I have seen the photographs of those aircraft, with sailors sitting out on the tips of the wings so that no cars or poles got clipped.

The carrier's ready room, which the Japanese had judiciously studied for fakery was, in fact, the actual ready room at Las Alamitos NAS. The studio had first photographed the whole room as they found it. Then they had completely disassembled it and brought everything—from notes pinned to a corkboard on the wall to pens, pencils, chairs, everything in that room—and reassembled it on a sound stage on Fox's lot.

Col. Paul Fennell had taken great delight in informing those Japanese admirals he was interviewing that they had talked themselves into psychological defeat because of a movie set built on a studio's back lot.

I urge all of you to watch Wing and a Prayer when it plays next on Turner Classic Movies, and see if you can determine if that flight deck is a real carrier's flight deck filmed at sea or only a movie set six feet above the ground on Fox's back lot. Enjoy the movie.

The Sweet Sound of a Baby's Cry
By Sydney Zelaya

The Labor and Delivery unit (L&D) in Naval Hospital Okinawa Japan was extremely busy. We averaged about one hundred births a month. I trained as an L&D corpsman[2] for a few weeks starting in December of 2014 and was on my own, assigned to rooms with a nurse, relatively quickly. It became routine for me to help take care of moms and their babies. If anything happened that I wasn't experienced with, the senior corpsmen took over and were involved with any emergencies involving mom or baby before, during, or after delivery. I stood next to them or in the corner and watched what they did, because I knew one day I would be the most senior on the unit.

On a Thursday around three in the afternoon, I left a room where one of my patients was actively in labor. She was dilated about seven centimeters, so I thought I could take a break and grab something to eat. I had started to get the shakes, as I hadn't eaten since six that morning; I walked over to the break room and began inhaling a granola bar in the five minutes that I had. A very harsh, loud beeping from the computer screen in the break room startled me. I looked up to the monitor that showed mom and baby's heart rate, where I saw that baby's heart rate had dropped dangerously low. I heard most of the nurses jump up from the nurse's station, yelling, "It's Room 5!" That was my room. I ran with everyone else. There were so many people in there. The mom and dad looked terrified. Everyone was talking loudly over each other. "Get the OR (Operating Room) ready, we're going for a C-section![3]" "I can't find baby's heart rate!" "Get me oxygen and start a bolus!" yelled different nurses.

My heart started racing. I had to take deep breaths to

---

[1] Corpsmen are enlisted medical personnel in the U.S. Navy. Corpsmen perform duties similar to medical assistants in the civilian sector.

[2] C-section, or Caesarean section, is a surgical procedure in which a doctor delivers a baby through an incision in the mother's abdomen.

gather my bearings. I knew what to do; I was trained to respond to emergency situations. The doctor quickly told the parents that we needed to go to the OR immediately. There was no time for good-bye kisses. I grabbed the admission paperwork for the baby and extra supplies I knew I needed for the delivery and ran back to the OR before the patient got there. Overhead, an announcement was made informing all hospital staff that an emergency was taking place in our OR.

The hallway towards the OR was crowded and loud. "What do you need? What can I do for you?" asked one of my coworkers. I told him to call the Pediatrics team (Peds) and grab the baby bassinet for transport after delivery. Meanwhile, nurses made phone calls to the on-call doctors, surgical teams, and staff on the Neonatal Intensive Care Unit (NICU).

It was chaos in the OR. There wasn't enough room for all the nurses. The doctor who was performing the C-section yelled across the room, "Everyone stop! Listen! I need two nurses, two surgical techs, one Anesthesia Provider, and one corpsman. Everyone else out or stand outside of the room!" Quickly the room emptied out to who the doctor had said could stay. I went to the warmer and got a sterile sheet. I was the individual who, after the umbilical cord had been cut, would carry the infant from the doctor to the baby warmer. My purple gloves started sticking to my hands due to my sweat. I experienced the familiar feeling of my heart in my throat that I always felt in emergencies. My heart raced, and I felt sheer panic. I was only nineteen years old, and I was the one who was responsible for that newly born child. I needed to calm down and concentrate. I could not doubt myself during that time. The life and well-being of this tiny human depended on my full attention and ability to recall knowledge on care for a newborn child.

I was multi-tasking what seemed like twenty things at once. I had to turn on the oxygen, get the intubating supplies ready, hook up a breathing mask to tubing, turn on the warmer, have the heat on, and have my oxygen-level monitor ready to go in case baby didn't cry or didn't have that pretty pink on his face. In my head, I was going over all the steps to resuscitate a newborn. Stimulate and get baby to cry. Crying is good. Crying means breathing and heart rate over one hundred. You have thirty seconds. If no cry, assess heart rate and breathing. Get ready to administer breaths and so on. Dear God, please let this baby cry.

I heard the word "uterine" being called out by the surgeon. That was my cue. I quickly unwrapped the sterile sheet and draped it over my shoulders. My nurse came over and made sure it covered my body well, to not bump into the surgical technician with anything that wasn't sterile. I finally saw baby's head being pulled out of mom's uterus, followed by his shoulders and the rest of his body covered in vernix. The OR was silent. The surgeon quickly cut the umbilical cord and placed the baby into my waiting hands. I promptly walked eight steps to place the baby on the resuscitation warmer. I felt like I was on auto-pilot. Stimulate baby. Rub his scalp. Dry him off. Irritate him to get him to cry. I finally got him to give me a small cry, but the baby didn't look very pink to me. "I need Peds. Or NICU! I don't care!" I called out to my nurse. I was really worried. "Please cry. Please, please, please cry!" I thought, while I vigorously rubbed a towel to his body. I placed my hand on his umbilical cord and took a pulse. It was over one hundred, thank God. Next step, listen to his lungs. He sounded very congested, like children do when they're sick with a cold. I turned the little one over and started tapping on his back, trying to get all the amniotic fluid out of his lungs. I suctioned his mouth and got little in return. My nurse came over.

"Do you know where Peds is?" I asked.

"No. I called the neonatologist[4] and he said he was on his way," she said, as I handed her the oxygen-level monitor.

The machine gave off bright red numbers that indicated the baby was having trouble breathing and getting oxygen into his lungs. I grabbed the oxygen mask I had on standby and began maintaining his airway and giving him breaths. After what felt like thirty minutes, but was really no more than one and a half, the neonatologist walked into the room and over to where I stood. I quickly told him how the delivery went, what interventions I'd

---

[3] A neonatologist is a doctor who specializes in the care of premature, ill, or newly born babies.

already tried and how the baby responded. He told me to continue holding the mask to the baby's face while he listened to the heart and lungs. "Give him a couple of breaths," he said. I did as I was told, and we all stared at the monitor. A loud piercing cry came from the baby, and the monitor finally read that he was adequately delivering oxygen throughout his body. I let out a deep sigh of relief. He was okay; he was breathing on his own. I felt an overwhelming sense of calm throughout my entire body.

I wrapped him up in the standard white with blue and red stripes, hospital-issued blankets that every newborn child in the country seems to get, but left his monitor on to ensure that he wasn't having any further trouble transitioning from his mother's warm womb to this harsh, cold world. I picked up the little guy, walked past the blue sterile drapes, and leaned down next to where the neonatologist was talking to mom.

"Here's your little one, mama," I said. "He had a little trouble breathing at first, but the doctor has looked him over and I'll keep a close eye on him, okay?"

"Thank you. Thank you," she said, tears escaping her eyes. "I was so scared when I didn't hear him at first."

"He definitely needed some help, Ma'am. It's tough for babies to transition from being surrounded by fluid and then to air in a short amount of time. I'll come around later when you're out of the operating room and look him over again. Congratulations again," said the neonatologist, and he walked out of the room.

I leaned in close enough, so mom could see and kiss her baby. I told her I was taking him back to the room where dad was waiting so I could complete my assessment. "While in the room, I'll get his weight, length, and a copy of his footprints so you can take them home," I told mom.

I walked out of the operating room, placed the baby in the bassinet, and started walking towards the original room the mom was in. I walked past the nurses at the nurses' station, and they all peered over their computers to look at the baby.

"Hi peanut," said a nurse. "He's a cutie pie!"

"That face better be cute, the way he had us running around," said a fellow corpsman, smiling.

I opened the door to Room 5, and the sense of relief the

father felt was palpable. I smiled at him and said, "Your wife is getting stitched up in the OR right now. She should be back pretty soon, but she'll be sleepy from all the medications that were given to her." I took the baby out of the bassinet and placed him on the warmer. "Come over and meet your son, sir," I said. Dad walked over to my side while I unwrapped the baby. I completed my head-to-toe assessment, and informed dad that his son looked perfectly healthy. I took his weight, grabbed a set of vitals, and made a copy of his footprints for his birth records. After about fifteen minutes, I wrapped the baby back up and handed him to his dad to hold. I left the room after telling him that I was going to go chart and that if he needed anything, I was just outside.

As I walked out of the room, I felt my heart rate finally slow down; I no longer had the feeling of impending doom. I had multiple things to do before I could relax, though. I went to move the hospital bed outside the OR, only to find that my coworkers had already done it for me.

"Guys, you didn't have to do this, but thank you," I said to my team.

"What? Did you think we were going to make you do everything? You had your hands full with the baby. It wasn't a big deal," one of my teammates replied.

Nevertheless, I thanked him again and sat down to start charting on the computer. My hands were shaking, though I didn't know if it was from not eating a lot during the day or from the adrenaline that was wearing off. As I charted, one of my nurses came to my side and asked if I was okay. My facial expression in reaction to her question alarmed her. She pulled me into an empty room, at which point tears started rolling down my face. I had held myself together for over an hour; now my emotions overwhelmed me. All the fear, relief, and happiness hit at once.

"Something bad could have happened, ma'am," I said. "I could have messed up or forgotten to do something."

"Listen to me," she said. "Baby's okay. Mom's okay. Everything went right today. Take a breath."

I grabbed tissues and dried my eyes. I went into the restroom and splashed cold water on my face. Everyone was okay. I thought back to my coworkers and how they truly helped out in the emergency. I was grateful to work with people who had the initiative to think ahead and complete tasks for me while I dealt with caring for the newborn.

I went back to my barracks room after the shift had ended and reflected on the events of that day. I was only a nineteen-year-old, straight out of high school, and I was put in charge of caring for newborn children. Before joining the military, I was adamant about getting my five-year contract over with, so I could go to college and study criminal justice. Yet I found myself, four months after starting on an L&D floor, absolutely loving what I was doing, and witnessing the beautiful process of the delivery of a baby. I loved being in the room, bringing them into this world, seeing the joy on parents' faces at finally holding their bundle of joy. I enjoyed teaching new parents how to change diapers, and bathe and feed their babies. Yet while I liked doing all these things, it took an emergency that scared me to my very core to confirm what I am both good at and passionate about. That day I decided to make the field of healthcare, not criminal justice, my career.

He Cried
By Garry G. Garretson

The videos of the active duty personnel returning home, and surprising their kids, made him cry,
Seeing the emotion and love for a returning parent, after months away since the last goodbye.
He was a hardened combat veteran himself but recalled the times he left his kids to deploy.
No father was there for their school dance or PTA, but the kids prayed for a safe rendezvous.
The civilian spouse must do it all, though counting on others in the same military pool.
For our veterans and their families, we should be thankful, for they must adjust and retool.

You know what makes me cry: Remembering those who gave their all to provide our freedom.
Those who faced fear each day, before the final event that took their life with a roadside bomb.
700K in the Civil war, 400K in WWII, 100K in WWI, 58K in Vietnam, 54K in the Korean War,
25K in the American Revolutionary War, 15K in the War of 1812, 13K in the Mexican American War, And 7K in Iraq-Afghanistan war.
That's over 1.4 million, equal to the population of the city of San Diego.
They gave their all. We should shed a tear, and a nod to the 7% who also served some time ago.

They were Marines, soldiers, airmen, sailors and coast guardsmen. They were also fathers, sons,
 cousins, brothers, sisters, mothers, daughters, neighbours and friends who, for us carried guns.
My childhood friend Chester Mollett, a road named in his honour, in the county where we lived.
It is hard not to cry when driving that road among the great Appalachians where we roamed.

Only one year my senior, he was a member of the 101st Airborne, leaving his job as a coal miner.
To boot camp and then Lejeune to prepare for combat, with others who were still only a minor.

He trained locally at Pendleton and then on to Vietnam. I fight tears each time I visit the base,
As I also remember the thousands who also served there and gave their life in another place.
Chester gave it all on 2/6/70. He was posthumously awarded the Silver Star for earlier actions.
The citation said "He single-handily assaulted the machine gun position, killing two occupants,
Destroying the weapon." His bravery saved the unit from the VC who had them pinned down.
My Uncle Loran was the preacher at the memorial as they cried and buried him close to home.

Boone County, West Virginia was our home and where families prayed, and served our country.
We were adventurers, miners, farmers, moonshiners, but mostly we were hillbillies to testify.
But many died volunteering to give two-four years in a foreign land, direct combat or off shore.
Taps played for many, before a return to family, while many saved other veterans live in war.
They were there to fight for our liberty, our freedom of religion, speech and press at their core.
Hillbillies make great soldiers, Marines, sailors and airmen on the ground, the air or the shore.

Dad was a medic in WWII for four years. My Brothers Bob and David served in Vietnam.

My youngest son is a Marine. Our uncles served in Korea and WWII. We did our duty afar.

My first cousins John and Paul served in Nam, receiving a Purple Heart and Silver/Bronze star.

We were taught to have true grit: the courage and the resolve to keep going until the end.

My uncles, one cousin, and my brother are no longer with us and I remember them fondly today.

Yes, I cried when they passed on as a hero. None liked war. None of them liked being away.

I try to lead with my brain, but the tears come when seeing military families reunited.
Remembering our veterans killed in action, or the memorials for our fallen heroes sighted.
Yes, I can get emotional, thinking about fallen warriors, those wounded who did not flee,
For those who survived combat, and all those who served in any capacity to keep the USA free.
Do you cry? You are the beneficiary! It is for your freedom that veterans do decree.
It is why some gave their life, and when taps play, we should be thankful, cry and bend a knee?

They were the best of the best, who died for a free future. They advanced our beliefs.

They protected our values, which have stood for over 240 years, through tribulations and grief's.

Let us voice solemn thanks for those who left part of themselves behind or never returned,

For those who paid the ultimate sacrifice for freedoms and peace, never to be overturned.

They gave back for what they had been given by past veterans, on whose sacrifices' we depend.

Share a moment of solemn silence for those heroes who died, so we can be here for every Memorial Day Weekend.

Special Liberty
By Joe Ashby

It was a beautiful fall morning in San Diego, and I had liberty from my Navy duties on North Island. My "kiddy cruise" was nearly over, as I would soon reach 21. I needed a day to explore San Diego, especially the zoo—something I had always wanted to do.

I took the "nickel snatcher" ferry that connected North Island to San Diego and moseyed up Broadway toward the YMCA with not a care in the world. That is, until two uniformed shore patrol swabbies came up and asked if I was in the military.

Being in civilian clothes and wanting nothing more than being non-military," I said, "no."

What happened from then on changed not only my day but also the rest of my life.

"Then," they inquired, "let us see your draft card."

You see, this was the time when all young men were subject to the draft. Now I was stuck; one lie couldn't be absolved by another. I was on liberty all right, but I didn't have a liberty card to prove it, and, as I was in the Navy, I didn't have or need a draft card.

In short order, I was arrested and placed in a "convenience" brig there on the shoreline of San Diego Bay. It was a small enclosure, only about six feet square, and the only thing I could see through the rusty short steel bars on the door was North Island Naval Air Station, where my morning's events had begun.

I hadn't been searched yet, but I panicked when I recalled the presence in my wallet of a bogus meal pass card. They were easy to come by, but the threat of a court-martial or at least a Captain's Mast if you got caught with one came to mind. Quickly, I took it out, swallowed it, and introduced it to my digestive system for fear of committing my second serious crime.

Hours passed as I languished there in my prison, the heat of the passing day increasing the level of my discomfort. Besides, I'd skipped morning chow to get to the zoo early, and the only thing I'd eaten since then was the fake meal-pass.

Finally, shore patrolmen showed up and had confirmed

that I was, indeed, in the Navy, had authorized absence from my duty station on North Island, and was free to return to that duty station on the next *nickel snatcher.*

It was evening, and I had even missed dinner at the chow hall back on North Island. On duty the next morning, my Navy chief smirked and shook his head but made no great deal of my ordeal of the previous day.

But I will never forget the loss of that day—from great expectations of wonderful sights and pleasures to exceptional discomfort and dismal disappointment. Eventually, long after I was discharged from the Navy, I had the opportunity to see and enjoy the San Diego Zoo.

So, what did I learn from that experience long before? What benefit did it yield to my life? Always tell the truth—and, if you can't tell the truth, at least tell a plausible lie.

The Case of the Arrogant Squadron Commander
By Lawrence J. Klumas

"When you hire experts, listen to them."

Stated another way: "Experts are those who have survived numerous challenges and finally achieved a reasonable level of wisdom. This story illustrates that truism very well, and it has solidified my belief in that piece of powerful advice.

My secretary, Kitty Bauer, put a telephone call through to me. If she did that, it would have meant that the caller was of equal or lesser rank or importance relative to mine. If it had been someone of higher rank, she would have popped her head into the office to alert me to the caller of higher rank before transferring the call.

"Hey, Klumas," the caller said, "welcome to Vandy. Got a problem. Know you can help me out." With no time given for a response, he continued, "Need a welder. Fifteen minutes. That's it. That's all. You can do that, can't you?"

"Who is this?" I asked politely.

"Oh, hey, Supply Squadron Commander. Been here for six years. Gone through three different BCEs. Been around. How's that?"

"Excuse me, and your name sir?"

"You haven't looked me up yet? I support you guys all day long. Seems to me you ought to know who keeps your squadron afloat. Chuck; name's Chuck."

I still didn't know his name, but Kitty, who had been monitoring the conversation, popped her head through the door and mouthed, "Colonel Charles Jones. He's a problem." I nodded that I had heard her.

"Well, Chuck, what can I do for you?"

"Just told you. Send me a welder for fifteen minutes. Need a small repair job. Nothing much. But need it now, right away!"

"Do you have a work request for this work? If you ..."

Before I could finish, he cut me off, "Look, we all need to help one another out, don't we? Don't need all that fancy-pants paperwork. I know what I need. How about it?"

"Well, then tell me the problem so I can figure out how best to help you."

"No need for that, Klumas. Are you going to help with that welder for fifteen minutes or not?"

I evaluated this terse demanding conversation. I could have insisted on more information. I could have insisted on a work request. I could have stonewalled him. But I didn't: I went along with his verbal request.

"When do you need him?"

"Let's see. It's 0800 hours now; let's just say, 1100 today. Is that OK? Or am I asking for too much, something you can't do?" His voice was now pushy. He felt he had won round one.

"Whom should he report to?"

"Whom? My, my, fancy word. At my office. See my top sergeant. Don't send him late. I'm a very busy guy. Need this little thing fixed right now."

"All right as you request," I answered and hung up.

I called in a sheet metal worker/welder. It was a good thing he hadn't left the shop yet. I gave him some specific directions and finished with, "when you have been there for fifteen minutes, I want you to pack up and come back directly to me."

"Understand," Technical Sergeant Bill Cliff said.

I had not been assigned as the Base Civil Engineer (BCE) (Director of Facilities Management in civilian terms) at Vandenberg AFB on the Central Coast of California for very long—perhaps two weeks. Just two weeks; I had hardly unpacked.

The Strategic Air Command (SAC), to which I was assigned, was the host for this special base, the Western Missile Test Range and Space Launch Program. The BCE was responsible for the maintenance and repair of all the physical facilities on the base. I had been in the Facilities Maintenance and Management business for over twenty years and felt I was quite competent.

At 11:30 hours, as the Tech Sergeant was pulling up to my office area, Colonel Jones, Chuck, was put through on the phone, "Your welder walked off the job. In fact, he didn't even start the job. He hadn't even unpacked all his equipment, and he just took off. I want to know what's going on. What kind of an outfit are you running down there anyway?"

"I thought we had an agreement," I said.

"We absolutely did. Glad you recognize that!"

"And you asked for a welder for fifteen minutes. Small job."

"Right there too," he said, and I could see him smiling.

"And he was there on time for the job, exactly as you requested."

"No, no, no. He went AWOL on the job."

"What job?"

"The job I requested." His voice was rising.

"You didn't request a job; you requested minutes. I gave you exactly what you asked for. Fifteen minutes."

He hesitated a moment, then said, "That was just a figure of speech."

"And I asked you for more information, so I could help. You said that was all you needed."

"Well, er, that's not the point. I wanted him to do the job I needed to have done."

"He did. We fulfilled your need."

"Well, that's stupid. Send him back."

"Let's see. I am looking at his schedule. He's not available for another three weeks."

"That's a bunch of crap. Let's go see the General."

Because I was confident in my action, I said, "OK, let's do it."

"Never mind," he concluded.

What I reinforced in my learning from this incident with the arrogant Supply Squadron Commander was this: If you have a problem with some issue, and you give it (or call it in) to an expert, let the expert figure out the solution. Only give him/her the problem.

Do not presume that you know more than the training, the hard-earned experience, and the insight of wisdom of that person. Listen to their proposed solution. Ask questions.

Follow the procedures, the rules. It is easier. It is the proper, the fastest, and unquestionably the best way to conduct business, whether military or civilian

Still Standing
By Vernita Black

You may say that is over for me, but I am still standing and happy
as can be
You may think that I don't have the ability to see
I am still standing and feeling very free
You may say that I am not beautiful or smart
I am still standing with love in my heart
You may say that I am old and beat up
I am still standing no matter what
You may say that I don't have a clue
I am still standing what can you do
You may say that my pain won't go away
I am still standing what can I say.

Crash Course in TeamSTEPPS

By Tanisha Wiley

Anything can happen in a split second; we all know this very well. On the other hand, nothing can ever prepare you for the opportunity to save a life. My first opportunity came in late August of 2011. I was a Hospitalman (HN)—one of a handful that came straight from surgical tech school—and the new check-in surgical tech to my first command, Naval Hospital San Diego. I had joined the hospital two weeks before, and just completed the task of Internet-based training. No one had yet paid much attention to me, much less gotten to know me. The looks of annoyance directed at me and the words spoken, as if I was non-existent, made it clear that I wasn't welcome. What was wrong with me? Was I not good enough? Was it because I was not as skilled? Did they treat all new people like this or just the lower-ranking sailors?

The morning of August 30, 2011, I was told to get ready for a major abdominal surgery and to meet with the Hospital Corpsman Second-Class (HM2) that would be my preceptor for my orientation. Filled with excitement and anxiety for my first surgical case, I stood in the office waiting for my team leader, HM2 Bert,* to take me to meet my mentor. He turned to me with a smirk and said, "You'll be paired with HM2 Smith to do a colon resection** in Room 1. He should be in the center core pulling for the case right now so head over, and he'll show you the ropes."

"Thank you, HM2!" I said. I walked out of the office and headed down the quiet hallway to the operating room that would change my life. I wasn't sure what to expect. I hoped my surgeons and nurse would be helpful since I was the new girl. However, I felt like an innocent lamb, being thrown to a pride of hungry lions. I opened the door and walked into the cold room, where I was greeted by the grumpy voice of my nurse, Lieutenant (LT.) Jacob.

"What do you want?" he said, gazing up at me from his computer with a look on his face that said, "Go away."

"I'm looking for HM2 Smith, sir," I replied, calmly scanning the room and observing how the equipment was arranged. LT. Jacob pointed to the door leading to the center core and turned back to his computer.

I poked my head out the door and saw a tall, lanky man stacking heavy silver containers on a little black push cart. "HM2 Smith? I am here for my orientation for general surgery."

"Great! You can scrub this case by yourself, and I'll help you get set up," he said, smiling as he shoved a silver container into my hands.

We both made our way back into the operating room, with the black cart stacked with six silver containers and a plastic bag filled with small packages of laparotomy sponges. HM2 Smith and I started unloading the cart and placing the containers on flat surfaces around the room, while LT. Jacob wrote my name down on a little whiteboard hanging on the wall by his computer. "I'm going to go get the patient," he abruptly said and headed for the big double doors to the main hallway.

HM2 Smith turned to me and said, "Go ahead and scrub in. I'll open the sets and throw up the doctors' gloves." I agreed, then carefully laid out my surgical gown and gloves to disinfect my hands and arms. I then reentered the room, gowned up, and started to set up my surgical table with the expert guidance of HM2 Smith. He gave me insight into our surgeons' likes, dislikes, and pet peeves. One thing stood out to me; they did not like new people. I became a little uneasy. "What have I gotten myself into?" I wondered. Just as I finished setting up my sterile field and doing a count of all the equipment, three surgeons threw open the doors and walked in, deep in conversation about the planned approach for the surgery. Their Captain insignias shined brightly in the light and caught my eye.

The conversation came to a halt as the doctors finally acknowledged my presence in the room. The female surgeon, Dr. Bailey, looked me up and down and then stared at HM2 Smith. "Smith! You're not doing this case! Who is this? I don't want her here!" she exclaimed. As HM2 Smith reassured all the doctors that he would take over if I made a mistake, I began to regret being in the room and contemplated asking to leave. The two male surgeons, Dr. Todd, and his chief resident, Dr. Riley, turned to continue their conversation as LT. Jacob returned with the patient and anesthesiologist in tow. As the patient's eyes closed and he slipped into unconsciousness, the room became much more active.

Everyone worked at positioning the patient's body in a comfortable pose and padding every joint, as I watched from a safe distance.

Afterwards, as the three surgeons quickly walked out of the room to go scrub in, HM2 Smith spoke softly, "Dr. Bailey wears the single size 7, Dr. Todd also wears single size 7, and Dr. Riley double gloves with 8 and 7½." I greeted and introduced myself as the doctors silently came back into the room, one at a time, to be gowned and gloved by me. The big blue drape was unfolded and laid over our patient, covering him like a king-sized comforter. The surgeons took their places, one at each side and one between the patient's legs. I took my position at the foot of the surgical bed.

The room was deathly silent as LT. Jacob cleared his throat and loudly called, "Time out!" He stood close as he introduced our unconscious patient, detailing his medical history, after which everyone else in the room chimed in and agreed that the information was correct. With all eyes on me, I nervously stated the procedure we would be performing and the narcotic medications I had carefully laid out in syringes on my table. The surgery started with Dr. Todd asking for a scalpel, and all three surgeons resumed their previous conversation of the medical plan. As I focused on the mumbled words of the doctors over the loud music LT. Jacob had suddenly put on over the speakers in the room, HM2 Smith whispered in my ear from behind, "I have an appointment. I'll be back later!" and swiftly left the room. I panicked. My safety net had just left, and I was stuck with three surgeons that didn't like me and a nurse who was either unaware or just didn't care. I had to hide my emotions and deal with the situation as best I could. I took a deep breath and tried to keep up with the demands of my doctors but also to get to know them, as we would be working together often.

Dr. Todd's voice suddenly boomed, "Towel!"

"What?" I asked, wondering why he asked for a towel.

"I need a towel," Todd said, exasperated, with one of his arms buried in intestines. I carefully handed him a folded blue surgical hand towel and watched as he unfolded it, stuffed it down in the patient's pelvis with surprising force, and continued dissecting through pink tissue and bloody vessels.

As time passed and the demands got more extreme, Dr.

Bailey became more annoyed with me. She yelled at me when I made a mistake, demanded I leave the case, and yelled at LT. Jacob that she wanted a new tech. I felt discouraged, but I did not want to give up. Even if I did give in, I had no one readily available as a replacement because HM2 Smith had abandoned me, and I knew deep down that he was not coming back at all. A few hours had passed since the surgery started when a cheery female nurse, LT. Campbell, appeared in the room to give LT. Jacob a lunch break. We went through a turn-over count and brought LT. Campbell up to speed on the case before LT. Jacob disappeared. I watched as the six-inch portion of cancerous bowel was removed from the patient and passed into my hands. I briefly touched it and looked at the delightfully pink piece of large intestine encapsulated by sticky globs of yellow fat and pulsating blood vessels, before placing it in a single bucket held out to me by LT. Campbell. Dr. Bailey thanked everyone, stepped away from the patient, ripped off her gown with one quick pull, and then retreated to her office. She exited so fast, it took me a few minutes to realize that she had gone, and I was left alone with Dr. Todd and Dr. Riley. The surgery was coming to an end; it was time to close the patient's abdomen.

LT. Campbell stopped her charting to come over and count my equipment with me, to ensure we had every piece we started with. Dr. Todd and Dr. Riley moved so quickly, I struggled to keep up while finishing my instrument counts with LT. Campbell. In the midst of counting the bloody laparotomy sponges, I stopped, as a big problem dawned on me. I began looking around the room.

"What's wrong?" LT. Campbell asked, with a concerned look on her face.

"We used a blue towel in the belly at the beginning of the case, and I don't know what happened to it," I stated, as I looked around the surgical bed, hoping to find it. I turned to Dr. Todd and nervously explained the situation regarding the towel. After vehemently denying any knowledge of it, he continued stapling the patient's skin closed. My sense of urgency increased, and I asked LT. Campbell to call Dr. Bailey, thinking maybe she had taken the towel out and disposed of it. As LT. Campbell made the call, I pleaded again with both surgeons to think about where the towel might be. LT. Campbell finished her phone call and confirmed my worst fear; Dr. Bailey did not remove the towel.

Dr. Todd and Dr. Riley gave each other a wide-eyed look, like two deer caught in the headlights of an oncoming car, and quickly started removing the staples and sutures that held the patient closed. I watched anxiously as Dr. Todd reached into the body and pulled out the bloody blue towel in one swift motion. I breathed a sigh of relief and quickly prepared another set of sutures. Handing Dr. Todd a new stapler, I resumed the count with LT. Campbell, which revealed no further discrepancies.

"Who is in charge? Who is the charge nurse? I need her in here now!" Dr. Todd demanded. LT. Campbell rushed out of the room and came back with the department charge nurse, Commander (CDR.) Grant, following close behind. Dr. Todd turned to CDR. Grant and explained what had just occurred during the case. "I want her commissioned right now!" he concluded. "She needs to be rewarded for what she just did."

I glanced up at the clock and chuckled nervously as I said, "I just want lunch. We've been in here five hours. How about a Subway sandwich?"

CDR. Grant smiled sweetly and said, "She will be rewarded, Dr. Todd." She turned and exited the room.

"I'm so proud of you," said LT. Campbell, with tears in her eyes.

"Ma'am, don't cry!"

"I can't help it!" she smiled and wiped away her tears.

The atmosphere in the room seemed to change at that moment, and a surreal calmness settled over everyone. I knew that I had just proved myself and my potential to be a skilled tech on the General Surgery team. I was overwhelmed with a sense of relief and happiness with the outcome of the surgery. Once LT. Campbell and the anesthesiologist wheeled the patient out of the room to recovery, I sat down and just stared blankly at the blood-soaked drapes on the floor. As I started cleaning up the bloody mess, LT. Campbell came back, ran over, gave me a huge hug, and then rushed out the doors again. Once I finished, I slowly walked down the hall to the break lounge. I could feel everyone looking at me and could hear the words of praise that circulated in the air. I had just saved a man's life, and suddenly opinions of me had changed.

The command was buzzing with excitement in the days that followed; I became the latest topic of daily gossip. I hated the attention. I didn't want to be known as "The Blue Towel Girl" or "The HN that called out a Captain." I kept my composure throughout that time, even when presented with multiple awards by my grateful department head and the gangs of Command Master Chiefs that followed my every movement. My peace of mind came from knowing that the man that lay splayed out on that operating room table was now safely resting in a ward room and preparing for his discharge, without knowing what an impact he had had. The operation had set in motion a change in surgical care and teamwork steps to prevent patient injuries in the Navy. Unbeknownst to me, during the surgery I had utilized a tactic known as TeamSTEPPS, Team Strategies and Tools to Enhance Performance and Patient Safety, which is the basis of optimum performance throughout the healthcare delivery system.

The TeamSTEPPS core is comprised of four main skills within a patient care team: leadership, situation monitoring, communication, and mutual support. These skills, combined with each team member's knowledge, attitude, and performance, demonstrate high competency and yield greater patient outcomes. At the outset of the August 30 surgery, I was not in a leadership role; however, when HM2 Smith abandoned his position, I took charge and made the tough decisions alone. I monitored the situation closely from start to finish to determine if anything had gone wrong.   Proper communication utilizes a Two Challenge Rule; the rule empowers any team member to speak up if they sense or discover a problem that may harm a patient. Just so, during the operation, I voiced my concern regarding the missing towel to the surgeons, more than once after my initial assertion was disregarded. My concerns were finally acknowledged, with the mutual support of LT. Campbell; her phone call with Dr. Bailey provided evidence that Dr. Bailey had no knowledge of the whereabouts of the towel. Had my sense of uncertainty prevented my speaking up, the patient wouldn't have survived. Because of the investigation that followed, Navy Medicine West implemented changes to standard operating procedures in operating room suites, and in-depth training in TeamSTEPPS for all Navy medical personnel.

For me, the experience was an awakening to a path of self-discovery and my potential as a valuable asset to the command. I no longer felt like an outcast within my department; instead, I developed deep confidence working with the surgeons, who before did not want me in their presence. I became eager to learn new techniques and easily memorized the exact needs of every new surgeon in my service. I developed strong working relationships with my team and was eventually designated as the leading tech of three surgical specialties. I was entrusted to share my skills and experience by assisting with the training of civilian and Naval surgical tech students. I tried to remain humble as I was continuously showered with appreciation from throughout the command. My mind never once strayed from the biggest lesson I learned: Do not be afraid to speak out when patient safety is concerned. Better that we voice concerns and be wrong than that we suppress concerns in deference to those superior in rank, and thereby lose patients who entrust their lives to our hands.

* Names have been changed to protect the privacy of active duty members.
** A colon resection is surgery to remove all or part of the large intestine. This surgery is also called a colectomy.

TET 1969
By Dante' Puccetti

I did not think I was naïve, but after I took my military oath, I realized I might die because some officer drove me to my doom.

The 1969 Tet holiday, the Vietnamese New Year, proved a disaster. It started on February 4th. The "powers that be" decided to remove me from the relative safety of base camp and move me directly into danger. I had driven convoys before, but on this particular holiday, driving a deuce and a half, similar in size to a moving van, my fear escalated. This particular vehicle had no top or back cover, leaving me completely exposed to the elements. The sun was a virtual fireball, and the six inches of Vietnamese dust-covered road settled everywhere gravity enabled, including into my every crease, making me sound and feel like a rusty robot with each movement. The enormous dust cloud my truck created camouflaged it from the enemy, but the engine noise would alert any North Vietnamese Army regulars who were nearby. Afflicted by the oppressive grime and by a cab that provided no defense from outside forces, including the countryside stench, the miserable climate, gas attacks--both nerve and exhaust--and enemy activity, I cursed my fate. I knew my unit would never have operated an uncovered vehicle such as this.

Carrying a load of cordite explosives from the Artillery Hill's ammo dump in Pleiku, I drove on Highway 19 to Ahn Ke, through the treacherous Ming Yang Pass. Suddenly the convoy stopped. Shots rang out and a six-wheeled MP wagon sped past, heading towards the fabled pass. When we restarted, the pungent odor of the nearby Montagnard "hooch" combined with the stench of warfare to overwhelm my grit-ravaged nostrils. I passed a tall, disoriented MP guarding the area with an M-79 grenade launcher. His distressed face bore witness to this fucked-up mission. I wore my helmet, but my flak vest was safely tucked under my seat to protect the "family jewels."

I left Ahn Ke and drove west toward Highway 14, then north to Kontum to deliver the cargo to FB Brigit [ZA015164]. I had hauled explosives around enemy territory before, but not during a major offensive. I was becoming familiar with the rhythm of the bouncing seat, the deep potholes, and the weird, triple-canopied jungle, which contained trees with huge root systems, vines that intertwined for miles, two-foot diameter leaves, and a damaged jet wing that had been caught in the upper foliage forever. The soft mulch, which sank to your ankles when you walked on it, accentuated the lushness.

I turned from a rough two-lane highway to a dirt road heading into nowhere. Triple canopy jungle concealed both natural and enemy terrors. I followed the truck in front of me. A thirty-foot dust cloud up ahead hid the leading vehicle, and my cloud obscured the truck following my dancing trail.

I headed west toward Cambodia and Fire Base Mary Ann [AS 961998], where I stayed with medic friends and the dispensary became my hotel. The great food and the bed were preferable to cold C-rations and sleeping in my cab.

Early the next morning, the empty convoy proceeded to a desolate area that had been "agent orangeized." I waited until a shitload of "flying cranes" helicopters delivered three batteries of 105mm artillery guns, one of which was slated for my truck. However, there was no way it would fit. I could tow the damn thing, but that sucker was huge. The gun was cranked down as short as it would go, but it barely fit, and my truck's two-and-half ton springs sagged in complaint. I looked at this monstrosity, with the barrel protruding into the cab, just inches from my right ear. I smelled the cordite stench of death wafting from the worn muzzle, and suddenly understood why the truck had no top.

I lost my bearings for a minute. Where was I? I was a sitting duck with a 10-ton artillery piece strapped to my back. I looked at the barrel and then glanced out the windshield up the jungle road. It was getting late. Time to get out of here! Urgency was an understatement. Stuck in a truck deep in Indian Country after dark, with my only weapon my M-16, was not wise. The jungle encroached onto the road, and the triple canopy enveloped the route like a tunnel, concealing the stealthy VC and bamboo vipers, better known as two-steppers – one step to get bitten and a second step to die. The tunnel was never brighter than twilight, but after sunset it became blacker than Hitler's soul. We departed as the sun headed toward the horizon. I followed the forward truck, but had a hard time staying on the road. We left the tunnel and rumbled over open fields and dust-filled roads again. Although I drove the hell out of that truck, it was all I could do to keep the dust cloud in my line of vision. But while that cloud obliterated all visibility, without the dratted dust I would have been a vulnerable target to the enemy.

I wanted to be anywhere but here. My heart was racing as I charged toward my doom. I prayed fervently to avoid an ambush. As I sped up to keep the forward truck's cloud in view, I took a curve too wide, causing my back wheels to hit a huge stump. Instantly the truck stopped, squashing me into the windshield as I bounced off the barrel of the artillery piece. Recovering, I backed up and steered around the stump to catch up to the disappearing convoy. Using all my racing techniques, I steered the swaying truck the best I could, but as I approached a sharp curve, the truck spun out of control and once again slid off the road. My heart was now running the three-minute mile. I gained control of the truck and once again set out to find the security of the cloud of dust. Sweat and dust was beginning to mound under my legs. Nam destroyed life in a cruel and unusual way. I wanted to turn north and drive over Ho Chi Min himself at that moment.

When I finally caught the convoy, I decided to stick closer to the forward vehicle, staying in the tail end of the dust. I was so covered with grit that if I'd knelt, you couldn't have distinguished me from a VC! Vision obscured, I missed a fork in the road, and suddenly I was driving on the side of a hill at a 45-degree angle. The road and dust had vanished. I thought the truck would flip. What a kick in the ass: Surviving Nam for eight months, only to be killed by a rolling truck. I instinctively turned down the hill to keep upright and slid to a stop. The other road went up and over the top. Where the hell was I? Which direction should I go, up or down? The wrong choice could be deadly.

Through the windshield, I saw the serene valley below. Though scared shitless, I was on this road now and figured it was good as any. I took my M-16 and lay it in my lap. I told myself, "Just keep on truckin' and catch the convoy." God was on my side. I caught the convoy at the bottom of the hill, and we arrived at the newly-constructed forward firebase where we dropped off the 10-ton artillery gun. Relief! By this time, it was dusk, and I decided to stay here for the night. However, the officer in charge had other plans. The empty trucks were to return that night to Firebase Mary Ann. That meant driving through unsecured territory during night, using blackout lights, in the middle of Tet. The blackout lights provided a low level of illumination for enemy spotters. Shit!

I could hardly see the truck in front of me to know where I was going. I had to ride his ass hard throughout that night's mission. Periodically, the convoy stopped, and I would grab my weapon as I heard the deafening sounds of the quad 50's on the gun trucks open fire, spewing out doom to the enemy. The quad 50's were so loud that they overpowered the M-60 machine guns and the rapid fire of the small-arms M-16's. Thank the Lord they weren't shooting at me! Once my lead truck went off the road, and I followed. I was thrown all over the seat as I plowed through 5-foot stumps outside of an old village. The Montagnard's built their huts on these stumps to stay dry during the monsoon season. What in the hell am I doing, driving right through a Montagnard village? I hope I didn't kill anyone; I never heard any shouts or screams.

I crashed through trees and God knows what else; nothing was going to make me stop. I cut the wheel, slammed on the gas, shifted to second and cut the wheel back again, over and over. I followed the bouncing red lights. I turned hard right; trucks appeared, and I felt relief. A miracle. I may make it through the night.

I made it back to Firebase Mary Ann late that night, exhausted, a state with which I was well-acquainted in Nam. There was always one more sandbag to fill, magazine to load, hill to hump, weapon to clean, grenade to toss, round to fire, horizon to scan, mosquito to slap, sound to agonize over. Yes, there was always one more thing I had to do to get home. Fuck this hole.

I learned never to be conscripted to wear a uniform, because in a uniform I lost my individuality.

The Beast Within
By Robert Caudill

(Read top-down as a combat vet looking at a caged lion)

Pacing back and forth as the beast within
I watch you without fear of death
Staring back at me, showing the predator you are
With the instinct of a hunter as our eyes make contact
Exposing to me how vulnerable you are as you try to blend in
Man has taught you with the lash demanding your obedience
You once had the heart of great lion hunting in the wild
Now you live your life among people
Hoping to return to a far-off land
Reminiscence how you were once feared and respected as you
listen to the welcoming cheers
You now have a mask you wear to show the crowds
How strong you are as anxiety overwhelms you
Only the like-minded can see your fear no matter how much you
pretend by showing
This fictitious side you're expected to display
As you miss the thrill of the kill
You are now confined to a world you do not understand
This is why I recognize your pain
It is through this way of life you are expected to turn off your
instinct
If only it were easy to turn off the switch
The few that have seen this way of life will understand it
While some consider you a beast, perhaps because they never
enjoyed the feast
When frustration is released in your new way of life
Some stay away in fear of your anger
Deep down inside I learned you are as vulnerable as me
In this moment of inner peace facing the animal within

(Read bottom-up as the caged lion looking at a combat vet)

The Shrapnel of War
By Leif K. Thorsten

To him he was a failure,
He could not face their eyes.
Many of them had perished,
So why had <u>he</u> survived?

Daily his mind would visit
Those who lay in their graves.
Daily he remembered
The brothers he could not save.

His loved ones and his friends
Worked hard to calm his fears.
His dog sat patiently by
While he tried to hide the tears.

Each day went on and on,
Only to turn to night,
Then, the countless fallen
Were never far from sight.

The memories that he carried,
Burdens, though never seen,
Every night they returned
To haunt his every dream.

Not even the passage of years
Could heal the wounds to his mind.
All the suffering and nightmares
Remained after all that time.

Why Hire Military Veterans?
P>E Performance is Greater Than Expectations
By Garry G. Garretson

I loved my military time and am forever grateful for the opportunity to have served.
What I received in return is still paying dividends, even when not being consciously observed.
We learned about structure and how to get the whole team pulling in the same direction,
Beyond each inspection and conflict, to choose viable options, as we always pursued perfection.
An "all in" attitude was instilled in each as they wrote the check, "up to and including my life."
Using a game plan and a blueprint: a target or goal focused on how to get there through the strife.

Rules provided boundaries, not to limit us, but so we would know how to initially proceed.
We did not waste time on things we could not change, while accepting the chickenfeed.
Physical conditioning became part of our daily living and kept us alert and ready.
High energy was achieved through physical conditioning, to keep us steady.
Doing extra was not extra. We learned to visualize a solution, looking to a Plan "B" or "C."
Pursuing the right reaction to an action, demanding more of oneself and others with spirit.

Working hard was not a wall poster, but how we knew we were protecting those around us.
We learned to show up on time every day with the right attitude, ready to work, a definite plus.
A strong work ethic was contagious. The military taught us to use every ounce of our "try."
Persevere was a drink that kept us going and gave us a never give up attitude stimuli,

Taking calculated risks with each operation, in the sky, on the ground or on the sea.
We followed orders and learned to conform, adjust, perform but never, never flee.

Being strong when it is difficult to find the silver lining, while in combat facing an armed force,
just patrolling the skies, oceans, or a piece of land, was a standard every veteran would endorse.
We learned to expect some hardships without complaining, but committed to work through them,
celebrating victories, not wasting time feeling sorry for ourselves, and not seeking to condemn,
Even when receiving enemy artillery in frozen terrain, in the desert heat or under the palms.
Being prepared for each environment was part of the job description, even amid the bombs.

Continuously pursuing job mobility skills enabled us to advance and get better,
Preparing for civilian careers through continuing education, even if by only a daily centimeter.
Equipping and empowering others became SOP as we prepared for war but hoped-for peace.
Vets know when and how to ask for help, when it is easier said than done and when to cease,
 Not knowing if we would get instant results for the missions, based on varying conditions.
We embraced change in technology, methods and experiences, but always valued traditions.

 The military is excellent at celebrating victories for individuals and for a unit,
with a genuine happiness for others while not resenting their accomplishments of true grit,
Always equipping and empowering others through support and training that could save a life,

Always being teachable was the lesson, but learning to be inter-
dependent, through the strife.
Continuously pursuing job mobility for the military life or the future
civilian career,
 ready for a new challenge, a learning experience, or the
opportunity to serve a new frontier.

We continually learned that those who think the glass is half full or
half empty miss the point.
The military taught us to refill the glass each day through
motivation, training and leadership:
Learning that character is far more important than giftedness or
knowledge, never to disappoint.
The art of obedience prepared us to lead, follow or get out of the
way but pursuing to conjoint.
Passion was a key ingredient to achieving our goals. Fair was based
on hard work and valor,
never dwelling on the past, looking in the mirror, but looking
through the windshield to explore.

Do you have a veteran's hiring policy? Do you know how and
where to recruit veterans?
 Do you know what skills they offer? Have your reviewed each of
your jobs to determine a fit?
There are several million with the testing, trials, and travail that
show they can continually do it.
 They understand the historical significance of their role. They can
look back at Valley Forge,
while flying a 2000 MPH airplane and understand that tradition
maters, but technology rules.
They know themselves from facing their fears, strengths,
weaknesses, dreams and passions.

They face the mirror in combat or while serving around the globe,
learning to interchange.
They know when and how to get help, and do not waste time on
things they cannot rearrange.

Military members earned their stripes and the ability to keep living while protecting the world,
From despots, dictators, terrorists, invaders and all those who live in the underworld.
They know their personal brand, learned in boot camp, during technical training, and school,
gaining the knowledge of how to deliver and how to align with organizations missions to rule.

A select few attended SERE school (Survival, Evasion, Resistance and Escape) instruct,
to learn in an enemy environment, learning the Six Article Military Code of Conduct,
in a real Prisoner of War (POW) environment, stuck in black boxes, interrogated, starved,
and stressed while learning to become one with nature, working together, eating rabbit's brains,
eyeballs and tongue to gain nutrition, and experiencing water torture for their rules to enforce.
Learning how to set boundaries, when to stray and when to know to stay the planned course.

I have recruited on many military bases, hired hundreds of veterans with great confidence.
Vets are comfortable with measurements, recognition, and getting subordinates conformance.
If you wish to build the best-fit team that gets results, hire a veteran who will not acquiesce.
"Coming together is a beginning, keeping together is progress. Working together is success."
Military personnel have their heart, body, and mind in sync to work together, and coalesce.
Do yourself and your organization a favor. When it is easier said than done, hire a vet.

Some did not return, some came back with wounds but most survived combat and danger,

Learning to use their experiences, to become better and the best they could be is not a stranger.

The military veteran can survive, learn, lead, develop others and get it done while others doubt.

They have proven it in circumstances non-military leaders hear stated or only read about.

Veterans prove that the best predictor of future performance is past performance without hints.

32 US Presidents, 80 members of Congress, 13 members of US Senate, 12 Corporate Presidents.

Veterans come with experience in HR, finance, sales, development and servant-leadership.

They are loyal and will stay, reducing the turnover costs and eliminating all the guff.

They practice the difference between just being busy and being hyper-productive,

Between just getting by, meeting standards or exceeding high-level expectations

Remember the difference they can make. You know they are survivors and paid their debt.

Do yourself and your organization a favor. When it is easier said than done, hire a vet.

Listen to the web site: www.verizon.com/about/careers/military
Veterans adapt, lead and deliver
They are driven, dedicated and knowledgeable
They have served and will serve with integrity and honor
They come with superb training, discipline and experience
They are strong leaders who help you stay competitive
They are the best trained work force in the world
Do not just thank them, hire them.

A Mountain of Fear (A Marine's story of Military Sexual Trauma)
By Stacey Thompson

"It's not how many times you get knocked down that count, It's how many times you get back up. "
George A. Custer (1839-1876);
U.S. Military

There is a mountain I've been climbing, on my way to the top
I can take one more step, but I just need to stop
To reflect on this moment, that has haunted me for years
"Military Sexual Trauma" is the mountain of fear.

The knot in my stomach is pulling so tight
The memories are coming back, regarding that night.
With all the mistakes, that fell through cracks.
Regardless of the details and all of the facts.
Nobody was comfortable even talking about rape
The room seemed to clear but, I couldn't escape
I was trapped in the undertow and gasping for air
They looked at me and said "girl, life isn't fair".

So;
Imagine yourself being drugged and then raped
Filled with the shame and enraged by the hate
Imagine your clothes being aggressively removed
Your lying in a bed but it isn't your room
You beg for him to stop but, he doesn't want to listen
He grabbed at your face and forced you to kiss him
He penetrates your body, though its against your consent
But there's nothing to do, as he does it again
The weight of his body has you fully pinned down
With his hands over your mouth, you can't make a sound
He's tells you to get dressed when he's finally done
But there's no where to hide, and no where to run
And your back in his car, not knowing where your headed
Imprinted in your mind and you'll never forget it.

The car comes to a stop; he thrust open the door,
It was a terrifying fear as I hit the floor.
He pushed me onto the street of Okinawa, Japan
Trying to get to my feet but I barely could stand.

I managed to get to a phone, I called someone for help
And when help arrived I described what I felt
But no one reports it and I had to be at work
Still covered in the smell of that sick, evil jerk
My stomach it trembles, and my hands fill with sweat,
This is the part of the rape, I wish I could forget.

But because I was raped and because I came forward
And because you did nothing, you decided to lower
The moral obligation you had, to even try and help me
Didn't matter anymore, because I was starting to see
That my admission of being, the victim of rape
Tarnished your reputation and kept you up late

I wondered what would happen if I decided to fight
Because all I talked about was how I couldn't that night
I couldn't fight back, I barely could scream
And this too was something that was starting to mean
That there in lie the possibility, I was seeking revenge
Angry because you failed, to help me in the end.

No one protected me as I went through this fight.
They left me alone like he did that night.
I was stripped of my title and no longer a Marine
For in the eyes if the military I was not what I seemed.

They told me the reality of what they perceived
I began to understand I wasn't ever believed.
Some people only focused on how I was dressed
Did I expose too much leg or part of my chest?
What was I drinking? How many guys did I date?
Am I really sure that what happened was actually rape?

They said I asked for it, by the way I carried myself
These were the very same people I turned to for help.
It's not easy to describe it by simply using words
So I'll articulate my voice to know I've been heard.

I wanted someone to listen and some someone to care
I wanted someone with who, I could actually share
The details of that night, I have locked up inside
When they come back to me, I again run and hide.

This is the story...of how I was betrayed
The story of the night when everything changed
The tale of the anger that was ruled by the fear
Doesn't even come close to what I want you to hear

Hear in my voice the pain from that night
Listen for the sounds that ignited this fight
Is it any wonder why, I kept this locked up?
Kept a tight seal, for fear I'd erupt
Back into the anger still fueled by hate
Because I am a victim of having been raped

And there is no consoling anyone, or making them forget
But there is one last thing that I haven't said yet
I survived the attack and overcame all the shame
Let this be a lesson, that it's time for a change.
It's not the times you get knocked down, that anyone's counting
It's the times you get back up and conquer the mountain!

A Faint Green Glow
By Charlie Wyatt

The night of October 16, 1966, was darker than normal, even for the unpopulated areas of Vietnam. A heavy overcast hid the moon. The Soi Rap River by day reminded me of my old stompin' grounds, the Warrior River in North Alabama, where I had spent a good portion of my youth. That seemed a million years ago. The boat I was driving now was a fifty-foot, all-aluminum PCF, popularly referred to as a "swift boat."

On the right was a long stretch of jungle with only a few tiny fishing villages, many miles apart. On the left was a vast swampy triangle, the Rung Sat Special Zone. No friendlies were supposed to be there; consequently, it had been labeled a "free fire zone." This meant that any activity was assumed to be Viet Cong and could be fired on. My job, as skipper of the boat, was to patrol the river, hopefully preventing any infiltration across it by the enemy. The river was none too wide at this point, and I wanted to be as nearly as possible in the middle, maybe 200 yards from either bank.

Up to that point, my life had been not just relatively uneventful, but smooth, for lack of a better term. I had a stable two-parent household in a quiet kid-populated neighborhood. I did well in school, and even in my teen years suffered almost none of the agonies often associated with that period. I aced the qualifying exam for a Naval ROTC scholarship to Auburn University and basically cruised through four and a half years there. Commissioned an ensign in the Navy, I spent two and a half years in San Diego, having about as much fun as a single young officer could have. I suspect that somewhere deep inside me was a feeling not only that life was good, but also that somehow, I deserved it, that the world had an obligation to make things go my way.

My crew of five was distributed throughout the boat. The boatswain and the engineman were on the rear deck, manning the over and under 50-caliber machine gun/81 mm mortar.

My radioman was in the cabin just behind me, while the seaman was at the controls, with me at his side. Above us in the turret was the gunner's mate, manning the twin 50-caliber machine guns. A few hours into the night, I told Parker, the eighteen-year-old seaman, "Why don't you take a break? Stretch out on one of the cots in the cabin. I've got it for the next few hours."

We were cruising at about 10 knots, roughly 11 miles an hour. The boat was capable of making 36 knots all out, but the engine noise was such that it would alert any would-be infiltrators a mile or two away, plus use up a bunch of fuel for the two 16-cylinder diesel engines. As it was, the quiet murmur of the engines was almost too soothing, especially at 2 AM.

I had made the run to the top edge of my patrol area and was now headed back down the 18-mile stretch that led first to a small bay, then to the South China Sea. I was concerned that the radio, never very reliable, had gone silent for a while. We were running without lights, of course, and I could make out the faint green glow on the dial of the radio. I had been more or less slouched back in the driver's chair but now I leaned far forward, my nose almost touching what in a car would be the dashboard, to try and adjust the blasted radio.

It is a fact that a bullet travels much faster than the sound of the gun it was fired from. Hence the saying: "You never hear the shot that kills you." What I did hear was the round tearing through the thin aluminum fabric of the door to my left, which gave about the same protection as a damp washcloth. The gunner's mate heard it, as well, and cut loose with the twin 50s. I was already pushing the throttles to wide open and as far as I could tell, we hadn't taken another hit.

About a half mile later, I did a 180-degree turn. When we passed the spot we had taken fire from, we cut loose with the 50s, and a few mortar rounds. We couldn't see anything definite to aim at, but at least we'd give whoever was over there something to think about. We had been shot at a number of times before and taken a few hits, so I was not particularly worried this time. The rest of the night passed without incident. There were even a couple of joking references from the crew as to how fast I had gone from moseying along to flat out sprinting.

Then came the dawn, not only in the physical sense, but metamorphic as well. My seaman came to take the wheel and glancing around said, "Hey, skipper, take a look at this."

"This" was the exit hole the round had made on the right side. It was obvious that its path from entrance to exit was a straight line directly through where my head would have been in normal driving position. I stood there looking from the ragged hole where it entered to the smooth one where it left. At that moment, my life changed. It was the coincidence that I had leaned forward a few seconds prior to the shot to adjust the radio dial that had saved me. I realized that nothing was owed to me and that whatever the world had in store for me, it would be smart to accept it, not as my due, but as a gift. I vowed not only to use whatever time I had left on earth to live as fully and productively as I could, but also not to let petty things--and most things are petty when you get right down to it--make any real difference. That was a long time ago in my eventful life, but that October morning definitely taught me a lesson which I have not forgotten.

A Day of Remembrance
By Shellie Hall

A warm breeze swept through the trees and around monuments honoring numerous fallen service members. The sun shone brightly as the American and Marine Corps flags flew silently in the wind. Chairs were precariously placed in neat columns before a podium in a small courtyard. Friends, family, and brothers-in-arms, embracing one another and telling stories, made their way into the courtyard where a ceremony was soon to begin. Conversations were nearly muted as the Patriot Guard Riders, wearing leather jackets and denim vests adorned with countless patches and pins, pulled into a nearby parking lot on throaty motorcycles to honor the fallen Marines of 3rd Battalion, 5th Marine Regiment (3/5). The Patriot Guard Riders is a diverse group of motorcycle riders from across the country who ensure dignity and respect at memorial services that honor fallen military heroes, first responders and honorably discharged veterans.

It was Friday, April 29th, 2016. I was tasked with photographing the 3/5 "Dark Horse" Reunion. The event was held to honor twenty-five Marines killed in action while serving in Sangin, Afghanistan, between 2010 and 2011, to honor those lost after the deployment, and to reunite those who are still alive today. I was told to expect a short memorial ceremony, followed by a barbeque and a hike up the legendary First Sergeant's Hill. As a young Marine, I became irritated because I was expected to work past normal working hours and complained about my Friday night being cut short. Little did I know that this experience would leave a lasting impact on my life.

I drove about thirty minutes to the San Mateo Memorial Garden on Camp Pendleton, California, with Corporal William Perkins, my coworker who was tasked with helping me learn how to be more independent in our line of work. I took photos of the Patriot Guard Riders wearing their Veterans of Foreign Wars caps and holding flags as they spoke with Marines, of friends seeing each other for the first time in years, and of loved ones as they made their way to their seats. When the ceremony began, the chaplain was asked to come forward for a prayer.

"Let us pray," he said, and the crowd bowed their heads.

To my left, I saw Jim Reed, a Patriot Guard Rider, remove his Vietnam War veteran ball cap with his right hand and place it over his heart while he clutched an American flag in his left hand. The moment of silence felt like an eternity as I made my way around the crowd, taking photographs. After the prayer, Colonel Jason Morris, who served as the battalion's commander during the deployment to Afghanistan, began to speak and the crowd grew silent. He spoke about the deployment—the laughs and hardships shared, the lessons learned, and more importantly, the Marines who served bravely. Chills ran down my spine as he read each individual name of the twenty-five Marines his unit lost overseas. As I looked around the crowd, I saw a father's head bowed and a mother shedding new tears for their son killed in action. Their pain reminded me of friends and family I lost over the years.

The end of the ceremony was near as Morris asked the Marines he deployed with to come forward to receive a challenge coin. One by one, the Marines shook hands with their former commander, each with a smile as wide as the Grand Canyon spread across their face. I watched in awe through my camera lens, capturing the moments as they came. The Marines looked at their commander with reverence usually reserved for an older brother or father.

The coin exchange concluded, and the crowd made their way to a field a short walk away. Poster-sized photos of the twenty-five fallen Marines were fixed onto a fence surrounding the field. I read the names as I passed.

First Lieutenant Robert M. Kelly.

Sergeant Matthew T. Abbate.

Lance Corporal Randy R. Braggs.

Food was served and enjoyed under a group of tents at the field. Marines kept a watchful eye on curious children playing with a variety of automatic weapons placed on display near a handful of military vehicles. I continued to capture the event while the crowd around me stirred with emotions—happiness, sadness, excitement and nostalgia. Talk of the past, present and future was constant until the attendees began to make their way to one of two places: the parking lot to head home or towards First Sergeant's Hill.

As I walked over to the enormous and unbelievably steep mountain, I saw its deep grooves and lack of vegetation. Sand and rocks rained downwards as the hikers climbed the mighty hill. The mountain seemed to continue straight into the clouds as I stood at its base and remembered what my lieutenant told me before heading to the event.

"Hall, don't worry about doing the hike," he said. "Just snap a few photos of the ceremony, the cookout and of people as they start climbing. You don't have to do the whole thing."

I looked up and saw the thirty or so individuals scaling the mountain, many of whom were the 3/5 veterans we spent the day honoring. These men, sporting all sorts of attire ranging from jeans and tennis shoes to Silkies (provocatively short men's workout shorts) and cowboy boots, were climbing this mountain to honor the brave souls, their brothers, who sacrificed their lives for their country.

The Marines' camaraderie displayed while scaling the mountain inspired me to undertake this climb with them. I desired to share in their sense of purpose.

Standing to the right of me, Perkins also stared in awe at the hikers. I looked over at him and said, "We're doing it. Let's go."

"What do you mean, we're doing the hike!" he exclaimed. "Do you see this hill?"

Before Perkins could finish, I put one boot into the sand and began the climb. He followed. The hike was brutal and by the time I was halfway up, I was sweaty, covered in sand and defeated. I had climbed nearly three hundred feet of the eight-hundred-foot elevation when I heard someone climbing up behind me and made my way off to the side to let him pass. Sergeant Marcus Chischilly, a rifleman who during the deployment lost nearly his entire left leg after stepping on an improvised explosive device (IED), was climbing this mountain full speed ahead. I was stunned by his spirit and motivation.

If this man can climb this mountain and not give up, why can't I? I thought. He restored my motivation, and I followed him the rest of the way up the mountain.

As I struggled to maintain stability in the loose sand, my attention was directed at my hands and feet. One of the veterans yelled, "Come on, female camera lady! Get up here!" When I looked up as we neared the top, I saw the crosses—twenty-five massive wooden crosses, each uniquely decorated. Numerous beer cans, bottles, and cigarette butts were laid at the base of each cross, in homage to the fallen comrade the cross commemorates. Gathered in front of the crosses, combat-hardened veterans told stories of their beloved brothers and shared tears of laughter and of mourning. In this moment, I saw the rawest emotion flicker among the stern war heroes that stood before me.

My throat clenched, and I felt tears fill my eyes.

Don't cry, Shellie, don't cry, I thought.

Out of nowhere, chants of excitement rippled through the air as the Marines saw their former battalion commander approach the top of the mountain. Soon after he cleared the top, they formed a circle around him as he addressed them, speaking to them as he once did six years prior in the heat and sand of Afghanistan. I listened intently, feeling honored to follow in the footsteps of the men who sat in front of me.

"3/5!" yelled Morris, with his Marines seated around him.

The Marines screamed their unique unit motto in response, "Get some!"

They continued this chant for a short time, and then after a few last-minute photographs with one another, the group descended the mountain. My tears flowed freely as I silently walked down the mountain beside Perkins. Not a word passed between us as we made our way to the car or on our drive back home. I reflected on the inspiring acts of my brothers, so far from home, to protect their loved ones, their brothers- and sisters-in-arms, and the lives of people they would never know.

Less than a year later, I was deployed to the Middle East. I never experienced combat, and phone calls home were easy to make and receive. Care packages could be shipped to us in the mail most of the time. Nevertheless, there were times of homesickness and longing for normalcy as each day fused into the next. There are no days off on deployment. Work is continuous. I missed my friends and family back home. Thus, in some respects, I experienced firsthand what the Marines of 3/5 experienced in 2010 and 2011.

However, seasoned Marines I'd deployed with told me of the life they had during their deployments around the same time the 3/5 was deployed in Sangin. The commodities and comforts we enjoyed in 2016 and 2017 were very hard to come by in 2010 and 2011. I thought of the men I met at the 3/5 Sangin Reunion. When not engaged in combat, they often hiked miles under the blazing sun, hoping that nobody stepped on an IED as they made their way to their next destination. And I pictured them during times of combat, running with heavy loads on their backs and weapons in hand, as gunfire and explosions sounded around them. Though I never knew my brothers-in-arms who lost their lives, fighting the enemy, I will forever be thankful for their service, and the sacrifices they made fighting for our freedom.

AUTHORS' BIOGRAPHIES

Joseph Ashby is a native Coloradoan. The military has been a part of his life since he enlisted in the Navy at the age of 17 during the Korean War. In the 12 years that followed, he served as an aircrew "twigit" (aviation electronics) radio/radar/ecm member, was re-called during the Berlin Crisis, and then went to Officer Candidate School. After time off for "good behavior," Joe tried the Air Force through the Air National Guard as an operations tech and rose to 1st Sergeant, Chief Master Sergeant, and Command Chief. He retired with nearly 30 years of service. Since then, he has been actively involved in veterans' services. He has also had careers in communications marketing, product management, firefighting, and over 20 years in training management with FEMA. A father of three daughters, Joe resides in Oceanside, California, where he still pursues military interests.

Vernita Black retired after serving 21 years in the United States Navy. Dr. Black served in the Persian Gulf during Desert Storm. During her time in the military, Dr. Black earned her doctorate in Education Counseling. Her experience in education led her to become an author. Dr. Black is not only a dedicated author but also a poet at heart. In her collection of poems, *An Inspiration of Life*, Dr. Black offers her perspective on faith and life's beauty. The poems reflect Dr. Black's personal and professional ups and downs--both good and bad. She has published two books: *Parents' Perceptions of Their Adolescents' Attitudes Towards Substance Use by Ethnic Difference,* and *Life's Reflections: A Collection of Poems -- Serenity, Peace and Faith.* She currently lives in southern California and hopes to become an inspirational writer helping with pain, stress and medical disabilities.

Kevin T. Byrne served in the U.S. Army from 1970 to 1973. As a Vietnam Era veteran, his interest in writing began in the twenty-first century after studying our nation's involvement in Vietnam and the Yom Kipper War in 1973. Currently retired, he enjoys cycling, surfing, and studying computer science.

Tom Calabrese is a Marine Corps veteran who saw combat in Vietnam 1969-1970. A prolific screenwriter and action/adventure fiction writer, he is the author of the novel *Some of the Best,* which is available on Amazon. His short stories can be read in thevistapress.com.

Robert Caudill grew up just outside Detroit, Michigan, and joined the Marine Corps when he was 24 years old. He served with HMM-364, "The Purple Foxes," for four deployments during 2004-2010 as an aviation ordnance, fixing machine guns and loading counter measure flares. He also participated in casualty evacuation, which resulted in his medical retirement in 2012 with Post Traumatic Stress. He and Erin Holmes co-founded I Journey, a wellness center that offers restorative yoga, sound healing, and more, free of charge to veterans, the elderly, and emergency responders, and on a sliding scale fee to the community.

Eileen-Gayle Coleman is the first female in her Naval family to join the Marine Corps. While at boot camp, she spent two extra months on Parris Island due to an injury that damaged the nerves in her left arm. She was able to recover and complete her training, becoming a Field Radio Operator. Eileen's time in service included one tour in Afghanistan. When Eileen completed her active duty contract, she went on to MiraCosta College to study kinesiology, beginning her journey toward a career in physical therapy.

SgtMaj (RET) Bernard Coleman is a Marine Corps Veteran of 30 years. He joined the Marine Corps in 1986, and served in every element of the Marine Air Ground Task Force. His combat history is extensive and includes Desert Shield, Desert Storm, Somalia, Operation Iraqi Freedom, Operation Enduring Freedom, and Libya. He began his career as an Infantry Machine Gunner, and ultimately became the Regimental Sergeant Major of Combat Logistics Regiment 15. The greatest challenge in his career took place in Ramadi, Iraq, during Operation Iraqi Freedom. While on this 2004 tour, his unit lost 26 Marines, and he was wounded. Bernard is currently attending MiraCosta Community College and pursuing a psychology degree. His goal is to counsel Veterans that are struggling with combat stress.

J. Randall Davis has a BA in English from Stanford University, an MA in English from University of California Irvine, and an MSW from USC, where he was enrolled in the Military Social Work and Veteran Services Program. In the six years since graduating from USC's program in 2011, Randy has had various roles in the Transition Assistance Program at Camp Pendleton. In addition to his career working with service members, he has taught composition at MiraCosta College for sixteen years. Randy edited Veterans' Writing Group's (VWG's) *Away for the Holidays*, and is proud to have played a part in the publication of VWG's second book.

Glen Foss served as a junior naval officer from 1966-70 during the Vietnam conflict. His duty assignments in the western Pacific included a diesel-electric submarine and a mobile inshore undersea warfare unit. After retiring from his civilian career as seagoing operations superintendent for the scientific Deep-Sea Drilling Project and Ocean Drilling Program, he taught oceanography and geology courses at local community colleges. He currently does some freelance editing and writes mostly fiction—for entertainment and "mental calisthenics."

Shara French served 20 years in the Marine Corps, retiring as a Gunnery Sergeant. Ammunition Technician trained, she also was a Leadership Program Coordinator, facilitating Dr. Stephen Covey's "7 Habits of Highly Effective People" workshops, prior to retiring in 2001. After retirement, Shara pursued higher education, culminating in an MA in Literature and Writing Studies from California State University San Marcos in 2017. Her published works include the poems "Growing Meaning like Bean Seeds," included in the university chapbook of May 2010, and "Molly Ann," included in the university chapbook of May 2017.Her latest published work is her Master's thesis, titled "Worlds Apart: An Evolving Woman, One Female Marine's Assimilation into

Patriarchal Spaces, and the Grief Coda, including Critical Introduction." Shara is a member of the Woman Marine Association, as well as a lifetime member of the Veterans of Foreign Wars.

Garry G. Garretson received his Air Crew Wings and other Air Medals serving in the United States Navy from 1965 to 1969 as a Second-Class Petty Officer. He flew transportation and early warning flights in support of fleet units in the Gulf of Tonkin and Southeast Asia from 1967–1969. His unit was part of the famed "Typhoon Trackers," which penetrated and tracked typhoons throughout the Pacific Ocean. He was an electronics technician and an in-flight radioman. Garry retired after a 40-year career with a Fortune 500 company, ARAMARK. Formerly a Marshfield (MA) School Committee member and Parks and Recreation Commissioner in Massachusetts, Garry stays busy as a member of several nonprofit boards supporting children, the Vista (CA) Planning Commission, and North Coast Church. He is married with three children and one grandson.

Shellie Hall was born in Chicago, Illinois, and joined the United States Marine Corps in July 2015. After completion of recruit training and Marine Combat Training, Shellie attended the Defense Information School at Fort Meade, Maryland, where she completed the required courses to become a Mass Communication Specialist. In November 2016, Shellie deployed with Special Purpose Marine Air Ground Task Force-Crisis Response-Central Command 17.1 (SPMAGTF-CR-CC 17.1) to the Middle East. There, over the next nine months, she documented SPMAGTF-CR-CC 17.1's story through her photography, videography, and print stories. Shellie currently serves as the Digital and Media Engagement Non-Commissioned Officer in Charge at Marine Corps Base Camp Pendleton Office of Communication; she is also pursuing her Associate's Degree at MiraCosta College.

Lawrence J. Klumas enlisted in the United States Air Force in January 1961 and retired from continuous active duty in August 1987 as a Colonel. As an enlisted man, he was trained as a GCA ground radar repairman; as an officer, he was in the Civil Engineering Corps. He was stationed at Tan Son Nhut Air Base in Saigon, Vietnam, when the Tet Offensive was waged. He has been writing since attending college in the 1950s. Some recent poems have been published in JerryJazzMusician and in the Episcopal Diocese Messenger.

Richard Meyer was born in Inglewood California in 1941. Richard attended Lutheran High School and El Camino College. He served in the U. S. Army 1961-1963 as a Military Policeman. Following his release from the Army, Richard and his brother Jack owned and operated a steel construction business 1963-2001. He moved to Oceanside, California, in 2001, where he pursues his interest in writing about history.

Johnny Olson was born in Chicago, Illinois, in 1970. In 1988 he was reborn in California, as a United States Marine. After surviving a brief, yet violent, war, Desert Storm, he hung up his cammies and rifle and picked up his pen and notepad, where he discovered his passion for writing. In 1999, Johnny, with a couple of other mad cohorts, started Mad Swirl in Dallas, Texas. After wearing too many hats for too many years, he now only wears a few at Mad Swirl: chief editor, webmaster, and host at Mad Swirl's monthly Open Mic night. Johnny's work first appeared in print in 1996 in the now defunct *Lip Magazine*. Since then, his words and images have found their way into a few online and printed zines. To name a few: Mad Swirl: Issues I-VI, Haggard and Halloo, 10k Poets, PAO Productions: The Open Mic Project.

Bud Parson served in the United States Navy as a corpsman attached to the Fleet Marine Force. He was deployed to Vietnam in 1966-67. After being wounded in combat in 1967, he was medically discharged from the Navy. Bud passed away in June of 2017.

Captain Ron Pickett is a retired naval aviator with over 250 combat missions and 500 carrier landings. He was the commanding officer of a squadron and a Human Resource Management Center. His 90-plus articles have appeared in numerous publications. Ron's areas of specialization are Leadership and Management development and customer relations, among others. He enjoys writing fiction and has published five books: *Perfect Crimes – I Got Away with It, Discovering Roots, Getting Published, EMPATHS,* and *Sixty Odd Short Stories.*

Dante' Puccetti enlisted in the Army and became an Artillery Surveyor. He was stationed in Vietnam at the HHB, 4th Division Artillery at Camp Enary, Pleiku, from June 1968 – March 1969. He received a BA in psychology in 1986, and then worked as a counselor, data manager, and research and statistical analyst in the Alcohol Treatment Unit at the Veterans Administration Medical Center in Loma Linda, California. With Dr. Michael Chang and Dr Paul Yamaguchi, Dante' co-authored a paper published in *The Journal of Alcohol Studies* titled "Split Level Validity of Treatment Compliance in an Alcohol Treatment Program." Dante' was a recent staff member at SO. CAL. (SCCA) NEWS. Part of his memoir was published in *Exiting Vietnam*, authored by Michael Eggleston. Dante' is a member of Eggleston's writing review staff.

Frank Ritter is a multiple-award-winning playwright, a novelist, and the author of non-fiction books. He was a squadron commander in the USAF Auxiliary, Civil Air Patrol, holding the rank of captain. He has been a private investigator (PI) in California since 1975. As such, he has investigated injury cases that have won over $500,000 for the injured parties, has provided enough evidence for convictions in four homicides, and has trained PIs all over the country.

Terry Severhill is the author of poetry that has appeared in a variety of journals, including *Damnfino, A Quiet Courage,* and *Soul-Lit.* He is the recipient of the "Art Young's Good Morning Memorial Award for Poetry 2016" (*Garbanzo Literary Journal*). His poems have appeared in five anthologies and are scheduled for publication in three more anthologies and several other journals. Born in the north woods of Upper Michigan, he is part Chippewa, part Scot, part Marine and ALL American. Terry enlisted in the Marine Corps in 1968 and served in a Marine CAP unit in Quang Tri

Province, 1969-1970. More recently, he resided in Vista, California, in San Diego County, where he wrote and read at several open mic venues each month. When not writing or loafing or gardening, he volunteered at a homeless/marginalized shelter. Terry passed away in December of 2017.

Colonel Joseph D. Snyder retired from the Marine Corps after 25 years of service. As a helicopter combat pilot, Joe flew 1,200 missions in Vietnam 1968-1969 and was awarded 60 Air Medals, including the Distinguished Flying Cross. He served as Commander of Reserve Support Units both at NAB Coronado and MCAS El Toro. From 1985-1988, Joe worked for President Ronald Reagan at the Pentagon. Joe then served as Inspector General for the Marine Corps Air/Ground Combat Center at 29Palms, CA. After retirement, Joe was elected mayor of Dana Point, CA, for two terms. He's the current Executive Director of Torch 1975, Inc., a 501(c) 3 non-profit to "Support and Serve America's Veterans," and is a member of the Advisory Board of Saddleback College Foundation. He is actively involved in the Veterans of Foreign Wars, having served as National Aide-d e-Camp of the U.S. and as Post Commander, All American Post 9934 Dana Point. He is the co-author of the book *Operation Dewey Canyon,* released in 2016.

Hal Sprogis retired from United Airlines after a 46-year career. While with United, Captain Sprogis flew a variety of aircraft, including CV-340, DC-6, DC-7, DC-8, DC-10, B-727, and B-747. He has also served as an Aviation Accident Investigator. His four years of prior service was with the United States Air Force, flying the SC-47 in strategic rescue operations.

Stacey Thompson enlisted in the United States Marine Corps at age 17. She volunteered for her first overseas duty station to Okinawa, Japan in 1999. Shortly after her arrival to Okinawa, Stacey experienced sexual harassment in her workplace. In December 1999, she was raped by her superior Non-Commissioned Officer (NCO). As a result of reporting the rape, she was retaliated against and separated from the Marines with an Other Than

Honorable discharge. Over a decade later Stacey became a public advocate for survivors of military sexual assault.

Although a disabled veteran herself, Stacey is also her husband's full-time caregiver. In 2013, Stacey joined Senator Barbara Boxer in Los Angeles where she shared her story publicly for the first time. Her powerful speech led her to be invited by Senator Kirsten Gillibrand in 2014 to speak in Washington, DC, in support of the Military Justice Improvement Act. Stacey graduated with honors and has a Master of Science Degree from the California University of Pennsylvania. She was featured in Veterans Coming Home, a documentary in conjunction with PBS of short films which depict the struggles disabled veterans face after coming home and reintegrating back into society. In January 2016, after four years of litigation, Stacey received a discharge upgrade from the Department of Defense which finally acknowledged her honorable military service and she is now receiving her veteran benefits. Her tenacity and perseverance is apparent in not only her character but, in her advocacy work as well. Stacey can gracefully articulate her experiences with MST and PTSD offering a unique understanding from both the veteran and caregiver perspective. Her success and commitment to advocacy thus far is certainly an indication of things to come.

Leif K. Thorsten served in the United States Marine Corps from 1968-1993. He is a Combat Veteran, having served in the Vietnam War during 1969-1970. He was an enlisted man for 13 years and an officer for 12 years, holding 13 different ranks. After his military career ended, Leif enjoyed working in various fields. He was a cook, a nurseryman, a Corrections Officer with the Western Tidewater Regional Jail, a manager with both Best Buy and JC Penney, and an assistant manager with a chain of retail golf stores in Virginia. At the time of his retirement, Leif was the Department Manager of the Custom Club section of The Golf Warehouse in Wichita, Kansas. He currently resides in Oceanside, California, where he enjoys building scale models, artwork, and, of course, writing.

Shirley Turner was married to a Navy Chief Petty Officer for over

40 years. She was a nurse and nurse manager whose specialty was Emergency Medicine. Shirley and her husband raised three children and were the foster parents for numerous children. Shirley's poetry has been widely published and appears in several nurse training manuals.

Tanisha Wiley was born in San Diego, California, in 1989 at Naval Medical Center San Diego. She graduated from Helix Charter High in 2007 and briefly attended Grossmont Community College. She enlisted in the U.S Navy and served as a Hospital Corpsman from 2010-2016, during which time she received two Navy and Marine Corps Medals of Achievement, two Good Conduct Medals, and the National Defense Medal. She was medically separated due to injuries sustained during her time as a surgical tech corpsman stationed in Camp Pendleton. Tanisha currently resides in Oceanside, California, and is attending MiraCosta College. She is pursuing a BA in Nursing. Her dream is to become a Perioperative Nurse.

Charlie Wyatt served in the U. S. Navy 1963-1967. He was deployed to Vietnam for a year as skipper of a Swift Boat. He has had a lifelong love for books and writing and ran his own used bookstore for more than 20 years. He helped found and still participates in two writer's groups. He has had several stories published in various periodicals.

Sydney Zelaya was born in Alexandria, Virginia, and joined the Navy after graduating high school. She has been stationed in Okinawa, Japan, and Camp Pendleton, California, as a Hospital Corpsman. Through her experiences in Labor and Delivery, Pediatric Units, and Anesthesia Departments, Sydney has discovered her passion for the medical field. When her contract ends, she hopes to continue her college education and enter the field of nursing.

ACKNOWLEDGEMENTS

It takes a lot of people and effort to publish a book. Of course, it takes the authors, many of whom are being published for the first time. It also takes editors, and we had four--Gail Chatfield, Randy Davis, Glen Foss, and Bruce Rowe--who devoted considerable time and energy to this project. What's more, owing to those editors' feedback, Veterans' Writing Group's members bring greater grammatical awareness to our writing.

Of special note is the inclusion of stories by Bernard Coleman, Eileen-Gayle Coleman. Shellie Hall, Tanisha Wiley, and Sydney Zelaya. All were students in J. Randall Davis' Fall 2017 composition class at MiraCosta College. Thank you for your contributions; we hope this will be your first steps in successful future writing careers.

Thank you to the **Veterans Association of North County (VANC) Resource Center**, who provided our meeting rooms and AV equipment.